PREFACE

TO THE STUDENT

There is a secret to learning economics. Those who discover the secret learn economics more quickly, understand it more deeply, and do better on exams than those who do not. The secret is this: Economics must be learned actively, not passively.

Passive learning relies on "taking things in." Merely listening to your professor, reading the book, flipping through your notes, and feeling like you "get it" because it all makes sense when someone else says it—these are the hallmarks of passive learning. While passive learning can work in some subjects, generations of students have discovered it does not work very well in economics.

Active learning, by contrast, works very well in economics. Active learning means periodically closing your book, closing your notes, and reproducing the material on your own. It means knowing how to *use* the vocabulary of economics—not just recognizing terms when you hear them. It means drawing graphs on your own, explaining what happens as we move along a curve, and what makes a curve shift—not just making sense of a graph when someone else draws it for you. It means solving problems from the ground up—not just following along as someone else solves them for you.

This Mastery Study Guide will help you to study economics actively. Other than this preface, you will find nothing here for you to just read, review, or "take in." As soon as you turn the page, you will be asked to *do* things—again and again and again.

Each chapter of this study guide corresponds to the same numbered chapter in Hall and Lieberman's *Microeconomics: Principles and Applications, 2nd edition.* Every chapter includes the following sections:

- *Speaking Economics* asks you to fill in key vocabulary terms when you are given their definitions;

- *Chapter Highlights* asks you to identify missing parts of important conclusions from the text;

- *Important Concepts* asks you to provide lists and brief explanations about central ideas in the text;

- *Skills and Tools* gives you practice solving quantitative problems and using graphs—plotting them, interpreting them, and drawing conclusions from them;

- *Practice Tests* offer multiple choice and true/false questions to help you decide when you've mastered a chapter of the text, and when you need to go back and review.

In many ways, learning economics is like learning to play a musical instrument. At first your fingers are stiff and even the simplest movement seems labored and unfamiliar. But with active practice—and more active practice!—things soon become natural and easy, until you can scarcely believe you ever had trouble at all. I hope this Mastery Study Guide helps you make that transition, and helps you become a "natural" in economics.

TO THE INSTRUCTOR

Nothing is more frustrating than inconsistency between a textbook and its associated study guide. I know this firsthand. Over the years, I've suffered—as have my students—with study guides and texts that seem to come from different planets.

In writing this Mastery Study Guide, I've worked closely with the textbook's authors, Bob Hall and Marc Lieberman, to ensure complete consistency in approach, language, and content. Indeed, the authors themselves contributed many of the questions and problems in this guide. From the beginning our goal was to make the transition from text to study guide—and back again—as seamless as possible.

ACKNOWLEDGEMENTS

Bob Hall and Marc Lieberman have written a gem of a text, and it was a pleasure to prepare this Mastery Study Guide with them. Their devotion to their subject, and to their reader, is inspiring. Andrew Lemon, my assistant at Vassar College, worked above and beyond the call to meet our deadlines—checking, correcting, and suggesting problems, and always reminding us of the student's perspective.

Geoffrey A. Jehle
Poughkeepsie, New York

Contents

Answers to Questions

CHAPTER 1

WHAT IS ECONOMICS?

SPEAKING ECONOMICS

Fill in each blank with the appropriate word or phrase from the list provided in the word bank. (For a challenge, fill in as many blanks as you can *without* using the word bank.)

economics   1. The study of choice under conditions of scarcity.

scarcity   2. A situation in which the amount of something available is insufficient to satisfy the desire for it.

resources   3. The land, labor, and capital that are used to produce goods and services.

labor   4. The time human beings spend producing goods and services.

capital   5. Long-lasting tools used in producing goods and services.

human capital   6. The skills and training of the labor force.

land   7. The physical space on which production occurs, and the natural resources that come with it.

micro   8. The study of the behavior of individual households, firms, and governments, the choices they make, and their interaction in specific markets.

Macro   9. The study of the economy as a whole.

positive   10. The study of what *is*; of how the economy works.

normative   11. The study of what *should be*, it is used to make value judgments, identify problems, and prescribe solutions.

model   12. An abstract representation of reality.

simplifying assump.   13. Any assumption that makes a model simpler without affecting any of its important conclusions.

critical assump.   14. Any assumption that affects the conclusions of a model in an important way.

Word Bank

capital	microeconomics
critical assumption	model
economics	normative economics
human capital	positive economics
labor	resources
land	scarcity
macroeconomics	simplifying assumption

CHAPTER HIGHLIGHTS

Fill in the blanks with the appropriate words or phrases. If you have difficulty, review the chapter and then try again.

1. Economics is the study of choice under conditions of _____scarcity_____.

2. Society's problem is a scarcity of _____resources_____.

3. Economists generally classify resources into three categories: _____labor_____, _____land_____, and _____capital_____.

4. _____Micro_____ economics takes a close-up view of the economy, and is concerned with the behavior of *individual* actors on the economic scene.

5. _____Macro_____ economics deals with the overall economy, and focuses on variables like total output, total employment, and the general level of interest rates.

6. _____Positive_____ economics deals with what *is*—with *how* the economy works.

7. _____Normative_____ economics concerns itself with what *should be*. It is used to make judgments about the economy, identify problems, and prescribe solutions.

8. To understand the economy, economists make extensive use of *models*, which are _____abstract_____ representations of reality.

9. A simplifying assumption is a way of making a model simpler, without changing any of its important _____conclusions_____.

10. A _____critical_____ assumption is an assumption that affects the conclusions of a model in important ways.

IMPORTANT CONCEPTS

Write a brief answer below each of the following items.

1. State whether each of the following questions is primarily microeconomic or macroeconomic, and whether it is primarily positive or normative. Don't worry about the answers to the questions—just classify them. (For example, the first question is a microeconomic, positive question.)

   a. If the price of compact discs rises, what will happen to the equilibrium price of cassette tapes?

   _____   _____

   b. If we raise the social security tax on wages and salaries, what will happen to total employment in the United States?

   _____   _____

   c. How much have pollution-control devices raised the price of automobiles?

   _____   _____

   d. Should the federal government use our tax dollars to support the arts?

   _____   _____

   e. What policies would help improve the average standard of living in less-developed countries?

   _____   _____

   f. Should less-developed countries like Ethiopia or Ghana use government funds to subsidize basic necessities like bread or milk?

   _____   _____

   g. Which is worse for society: a one percentage-point rise in the unemployment rate, or a one percentage-point rise in the inflation rate?

   _____   _____

2. Each of the following is an example of one of the three categories of resources. In the blanks, identify the categories.

   a. A surgeon's time in performing an operation _____

   b. The surgeon's scalpel _____

   c. The surgeon's skills and training _____

   d. The iron ore used to make steel _____

   e. The workers who make steel out of iron ore _____

   f. The factory in which iron ore is made into steel _____

   g. The services performed by a waiter at a restaurant _____

   h. A restaurant's pots, pans and dishes _____

Indicate whether the following statements are true or false, and then explain briefly.

3. "The more details we include in a model, the better the model will work."

4. Economists make two types of assumptions in their economics models: positive assumptions and normative assumptions.

SKILLS AND TOOLS

Note to the Student: Some of the basic principles of graphs and graphing are reviewed in the Appendix to Chapter 1 in your text. If it has been a while since you used graphs you might want to take a look at that section of the text before you do these exercises. Those already comfortable with graphs can proceed with the exercises.

For each of the following items, write the correct answer in the blank or circle the correct answer.

1. This table reports estimates of the United States' population (in millions) each year during the 1980s. The data are population in millions by year.

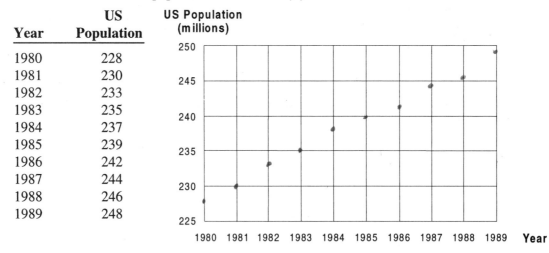

Year	US Population
1980	228
1981	230
1982	233
1983	235
1984	237
1985	239
1986	242
1987	244
1988	246
1989	248

a. On the axes provided, carefully plot the data from the table.

b. Looking at your graph in (1), which of the following best describes how population changed in the 1980s? ____iv____
   i. Population generally decreased over the decade.
   ii. Population stayed roughly constant over the decade.
   iii. Population increased and decreased erratically over the decade.
   iv. Population increased at a roughly constant rate over the decade.

c. On your graph for (1) use a ruler and draw in a single straight line which seems to best fit the data you plotted.

d. Slope measures the rate of change in the y-axis variable for a one unit change in the x-axis variable. Bearing this in mind, what is the rate at which population changed over the decade of the 1980s? _2.24 million_

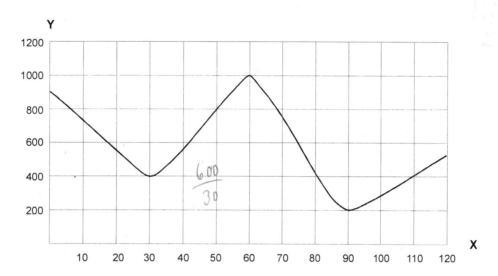

2. Study the graph in the preceding figure.

a. In the figure, Y increases when X increases from _30_ to _60_, and then again when X increases from _90_ to _120_. In these two regions, the slope of the relationship between X and Y is (**positive**/negative/zero).

b. In the same figure, Y decreases when X increases from _0_ to _30_, and then again when X increases from _60_ to _90_. In these two regions, the slope of the relationship between X and Y is (positive/**negative**/zero).

c. Y reaches its maximum value of _1000_ when X has the value _60_. Y reaches its minimum value of _200_ when X has the value _90_.

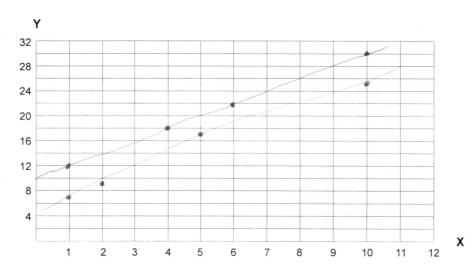

3. Graph each of the following equations on the grid provided. Then describe your graph by filling in the blanks.

   a. Y = 2X + 10

      This graph has a vertical intercept of _____10_____ and a constant slope of _____2_____. As X increases, Y always (increases/decreases) at a (constant/changing) rate.

   b. Y = 2X + 5

      This graph has a vertical intercept of _____5_____ and a constant slope of _____2_____. As X increases, Y always (increases/decreases) at a (constant/changing) rate.

   c. Y = X + 10

      This graph has a vertical intercept of _____ and a constant slope of _____. As X increases, Y always (increases/decreases) at a (constant/changing) rate.

   d. Y = 30 – 5X

      This graph has a vertical intercept of _____ and a constant slope of _____. As X increases, Y always (increases/decreases) at a (constant/changing) rate.

   e. Y = 30 – 3X

      This graph has a vertical intercept of _____ and a constant slope of _____. As X increases, Y always (increases/decreases) at a (constant/changing) rate.

10-MINUTE PRACTICE TEST

Set a timer, giving yourself just ten minutes to answer all of the following questions. To see what you *really* know and remember, take the test at least a day *after* you've read the chapter in the text and completed the exercises in this study guide.

Multiple Choice: Circle the letter in front of the single best answer.

1. Economics can be defined as the study of
   a. business firms and how they can increase their profit.
   b. financial markets, like the stock market and the bond market.
   c. choice under conditions of scarcity.
   d. how households allocate their income to different uses.
   e. how businesses and government agencies allocate their revenue to different uses.

2. *Micro*economics studies the economic behavior of
   a. very small nations.
   b. very small people.
   c. individual businesses only.
   d. individual households only.
   e. individual decision-makers, including households and businesses.

3. Which of the following is a *resource,* from society's point of view?
   a. Meat
   b. Clothing
   c. The income tax
   d. An office building
   e. Electricity

4. Regardless of its truth or falsehood, the statement "A tax cut will cause faster growth in total output than an increase in government spending" is an example of
   a. positive microeconomics.
   b. positive macroeconomics.
   c. normative microeconomics.
   d. normative macroeconomics.
   e. none of the above.

5. Which of the following is the best example of a *model*?
   a. A dollar bill
   b. A coffee cup
   c. A drawing of a house
   d. A stop sign
   e. A laptop computer

6. The best way to study economics is
   a. *passively*, reading the book over and over again until you can follow the logical flow.
   b. *actively*, making sure you can reproduce the material on your own.
   c. with a phone in one hand and a remote control in the other.
   d. bent at the waist, making a 90-degree angle with your upper torso.
   e. with Country-and-Western music in the background.

True/False: For each of the following statements, circle T if the statement is true or F if the statement is false.

T   F   1. All assumptions in an economic model are *simplifying* assumptions.

T   F   2. Economists classify resources into three categories: labor, physical capital and human capital.

T   F   3. Normative economics deals with how the economy normally functions in ordinary times.

T   F   4. In economics, we assume that individuals face scarcities of time and spending power.

T   F   5. *Macro*economics studies the economies of large, industrialized nations, such as the United States or Japan.

CHAPTER 2

SCARCITY, CHOICE, AND ECONOMIC SYSTEMS

SPEAKING ECONOMICS

Fill in each blank with the appropriate word or phrase from the list provided in the word bank. (For a challenge, fill in as many blanks as you can *without* using the word bank.)

Opportunity cost 1. What we sacrifice when taking an action.

PPF 2. A curve showing all combinations of two goods that can be produced with the resources and technology currently available.

law of increasing opp. cost 3. The more of something we produce, the more we must sacrifice to produce one more unit.

product inefficiency 4. A situation in which we could produce more of one good without sacrificing production of any other good.

specialization 5. A method of production in which each person concentrates on a limited number of activities.

exchange 6. The act of trading with others to obtain what we desire.

abso. advan. 7. The ability to produce a good or service using *fewer resources* than other producers use.

comp. advan. 8. The ability to produce a good or service at a *lower opportunity cost* than other producers.

resource allocation 9. The determination of which goods and services are produced, how they are produced, and who gets them.

traditional economy 10. An economy in which resources are allocated according to long-lived practices from the past.

Command & Centrally Planned 11. Two names for an economic system in which resources are allocated according to explicit instructions from a central authority.

market economy 12. An economic system in which resources are allocated through individual decision making.

market 13. A group of buyers and sellers with the potential to trade with one another.

price 14. The amount of money that must be paid to a seller to obtain a good or service.

communism 15. Communal ownership of most resources.

socialism 16. State ownership of most resources.

capitalism 17. Private ownership of most resources.

economic system 18. A system of resource allocation and resource ownership.

Word Bank

absolute advantage

capitalism

centrally planned economy

command economy

communism

comparative advantage

economic system

exchange

law of increasing opportunity cost

market

market economy

opportunity cost

price

production possibilities frontier (PPF)

resource allocation

socialism

specialization

productive inefficiency

traditional economy

CHAPTER HIGHLIGHTS

Fill in the blanks with the appropriate words or phrases. If you have difficulty, review the chapter and then try again.

1. The _____ of any choice is all that we give up when we make that choice.

2. All production carries an _____: to produce more of one thing, society must shift _____ away from producing something else.

3. The law of _____ opportunity cost tells us that the more of something we produce, the _____ is the opportunity cost of producing still more.

4. A firm, industry or an entire economy is productively _____ if it could produce more of some good without pulling resources from the production of any other good.

5. _____ and _____ enable us to enjoy greater production and higher living standards than would otherwise be possible. As a result, all economies exhibit high degrees of _____ and _____.

6. A person has a (an) _____ in producing some good if he or she can produce it using fewer resources than another person can.

7. A person has a (an) _____ in producing some good if he or she can produce it with a smaller opportunity cost than some other person can.

8. Total production of every good or service will be greatest when individuals specialize according to their _____.

9. In a _____ economy, resources are allocated by explicit instructions from some higher authority.

10. In a _____ economy, resources are allocated through individual decision making.

IMPORTANT CONCEPTS

Write a brief answer below each of the following questions.

1. Indicate whether the following statement is true or false, and then explain briefly: To determine the opportunity cost of a year of college, we would add the direct money cost and the income foregone. Thus, for someone who could have earned $30,000 as a full-time fisherman during the year, or $45,000 as a full-time truck driver that year, or $20,000 as a full-time tour guide that year, the opportunity cost would be the direct money cost plus a total income foregone of $30,000 + $45,000 + $20,000 = $95,000."

2. What economic law gives the production possibilities frontier its characteristic concave (upside-down bowl) shape?

law of increasing opportunity cost

3. Name two types of economic situations in which a "free lunch" for society might be possible.

    a.

    b.

4. List three separate reasons why specialization and exchange can lead to increased production.

    a.

    b.

    c.

5. College professors can usually locate books and articles in their college library faster than students. Yet most college professors hire students to find these materials. Is this consistent with the idea of comparative advantage? Briefly, why or why not?

6. List the three methods of resource allocation.

    a.

    b.

    c.

7. List the three methods of resource ownership.

    a.

    b.

    c.

8. List the four major types of economic systems. For each system, identify the method of resource allocation and how resources are owned.

a.

b.

c.

d.

SKILLS AND TOOLS

For each of the following items, follow the instructions, write the correct answer in the blank, or circle the correct answer.

1. By using its existing resources efficiently, an island society can produce the following alternative combinations of mangoes and oranges each day.

	Daily Production of:	
	Mangoes	**Oranges**
A	0	50
B	5	49
C	10	46
D	15	40
E	20	30
F	25	0

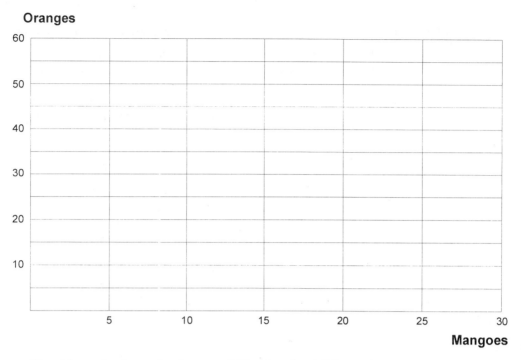

a. Plot this society's production possibility frontier (PPF) on the axes provided. Label the points A–F on your graph.

b. Assume the islanders are currently producing at point A, devoting all their resources to orange production. In moving to point B, this society gives up _____ orange(s). The resources released from producing oranges are then able to produce _____ mangoes. The opportunity cost to society of these first _____ mangoes is _____ orange(s).

Starting at point B, this society can move to point C and produce an additional _____ mangoes only if it foregoes an additional _____ oranges. The opportunity cost of the additional mangoes obtained in moving from B to C is an additional _____ oranges foregone.

In moving from C to D, the opportunity cost of _____ additional mangoes is _____ more oranges. In moving from D to E, the opportunity cost of _____ more mangoes is _____ more oranges. In moving from E to F, the opportunity cost of _____ more mangoes is _____ more oranges.

Moving along the PPF from A to F, the opportunity cost of mangoes is (increasing/decreasing/constant) as more and more mangoes are produced.

c. Now assume the islanders are currently producing at point F, devoting all their resources to mango production. In moving to point E, this society gives up _____ mangoes. The resources released from producing these mangoes are then able to produce _____ oranges. The opportunity cost to society of these first _____ oranges is _____ mangoes.

Starting at point E, this society can move to point D and produce an additional _____ oranges only if it foregoes an additional _____ mangoes. The opportunity cost of the additional oranges obtained in moving from E to D is an additional _____ mangoes foregone.

In moving from D to C, the opportunity cost of _____ additional oranges is _____ more mangoes. In moving from C to B, the opportunity cost of _____ more oranges is _____ more mangoes.

Moving along the PPF from F to A, the opportunity cost of oranges is (increasing/decreasing/constant) as more and more oranges are produced.

2. On the PPF above, plot the point representing total production of 10 mangoes and 30 oranges. Label this point G. Plot the point representing production of 15 mangoes and 50 oranges. Label this point H.

a. At point G, the islanders (are/are not) using all their resources efficiently. Starting from point G, the opportunity cost of an additional 5 mangoes would be _____ oranges. The opportunity cost of an additional 5 oranges would be _____ mangoes. At point G, does this society achieve technical efficiency (yes/no)?

b. The point H represents a combination of mango and orange production that this society (can/cannot) achieve with existing resources. To achieve point H, the technology of production will have to (improve/decline/remain the same) or society will have to (acquire more/use less) resources.

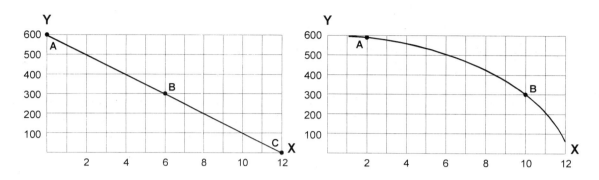

3. In the panel on the left above, the absolute value of the PPF's slope is (constant/increasing/ decreasing) as we move from A to B. Starting at A, the opportunity cost of the first unit of good X will be _____ units of (X/Y). Starting at B, the opportunity cost of one more unit of X will be _____ units of (X/Y). If we begin at point C, the opportunity cost of one more unit of X will be _____ units of (X/Y). With this PPF, as we move from A to B to C, the opportunity cost of additional units of X is (constant/increasing/decreasing).

4. In the panel on the right above, as we move from point A to point B, the absolute value of the PPF's slope (remains constant/increases/decreases). At point A, the opportunity cost of an additional unit of X is (the same as/greater than/less than) the opportunity cost of an additional unit of X at point B. At the same time, at point A the opportunity cost of an additional unit of Y is (the same as/greater than/less than) the opportunity cost of an additional unit of Y at point B.

5. Each entry in the following table gives the number of hours it takes a typical worker in the given country to produce one unit of the indicated good. Thus, it takes a worker in Norway two hours to produce one sweater, and four hours to catch a fish, and so forth.

	Sweaters	**Fish**
Norway	2 hours	4 hours
Sweden	6 hours	2 hours

a. From these data, we can see that Norway has an absolute advantage in producing (sweaters/fish/both goods/neither good). At the same time, Sweden has an absolute advantage in producing (sweaters/fish/both goods/neither good).

b. From these same data, we can see that the opportunity cost of producing a fish in Norway is _____ sweater(s). The opportunity cost of producing a fish in Sweden is _____ sweater(s). From this we can conclude that Sweden has a comparative advantage in producing (sweaters/fish/both goods/neither good), while Norway has a comparative advantage in producing (sweaters/fish/both goods/neither good).

15-MINUTE PRACTICE TEST

Set a timer, giving yourself just 15 minutes to answer all of the following questions. To see what you *really* know and remember, take the test at least a day *after* you've read the chapter in the text and completed the exercises in this study guide.

Multiple Choice: Circle the letter in front of the single best answer.

1. The opportunity cost of any choice is
   a. the money given up for that choice.
   b. the time given up for that choice.
   c. what is actually sacrificed to make that choice.
   d. how much you would pay to make that choice.
   e. how much you would pay to avoid that choice.

2. For society, opportunity cost arises because of a scarcity of
   a. technology.
   b. land.
   c. money.
   d. resources.
   e. markets.

3. As we move rightward along a production possibilities frontier, we also move
   a. downward, and the frontier becomes steeper.
   b. downward, and the frontier becomes flatter.
   c. upward, and the frontier becomes steeper.
   d. upward, and the frontier becomes flatter.
   e. neither upward nor downward, and the slope of the frontier remains unchanged.

4. A point inside a production possibilities frontier might represent
   a. productive efficiency.
   b. a recession.
   c. a situation of very high opportunity cost.
   d. full employment of resources.
   e. none of the above.

5. The production possibilities frontier is concave shaped (like an upside-down bowl) because of
   a. the scarcity of resources.
   b. the law of increasing opportunity cost.
   c. productive inefficiency.
   d. absolute advantage.
   e. none of the above.

6. Which of the following is consistent with specialization according to comparative advantage?

    a. Famous attorney Alan Dershowitz prepares and addresses his own bills and takes them to the post office each day.
    b. John Travolta walks his own dog.
    c. The President of the United States drafts his own speeches.
    d. All of the above.
    e. None of the above.

7. One reason why specialization and exchange lead to greater production is

    a. comparative advantage.
    b. the development of expertise.
    c. the time saving from not having to switch tasks.
    d. all of the above.
    e. none of the above.

8. Which of the following is a method of resource allocation?

    a. Capitalism
    b. Socialism
    c. Command
    d. All of the above
    e. None of the above

9. Resource allocation involves an answer to which of the following questions?

    a. How are the economy's goods and services produced?
    b. What determines the rate of unemployment?
    c. How can business firms increase their profit?
    d. All of the above.
    e. None of the above.

10. Under *market capitalism*, resources are

    a. owned by society as a whole.
    b. owned by the market itself.
    c. owned by no one.
    d. allocated in an entirely random way.
    e. none of the above.

True/False: For each of the following statements, circle T if the statement is true or F if the statement is False.

T   F   1. The correct measure of the cost of a choice is the time used up by that choice.

T   F   2. The law of increasing opportunity cost tells us that the opportunity costs of our choices tend to rise over time.

T   F   3. If we can produce more of one good without producing less of any other goods, the economy is productively inefficient.

T   F   4. An individual has a comparative advantage in producing a good if he or she can produce it at a lower opportunity cost than some other individual.

T   F   5. The United States is an example of a pure market economy, in which all resource allocation is accomplished through the market.

T   F   6. An economic system is comprised of two components: a system of resource allocation and a system of resource ownership.

T   F   7. A recession can be illustrated by a movement downward and rightward along a country's production possibilities frontier.

T   F   8. The economic system of the former Soviet Union was market socialism.

CHAPTER 3

SUPPLY AND DEMAND

Fill in the blank with the appropriate word or phrase from the list provided in the word bank. (For a challenge, fill in as many blanks as you can *without* using the word bank.)

_____ 1. The process of combining distinct things into a single whole.

_____ 2. A market in which a single buyer or seller has the power to influence the price of the product.

_____ 3. A market in which *no* buyer or seller has the power to influence the price of the product.

_____ 4. The total amount of a good an individual would choose to purchase at a given price.

_____ 5. The total amount of a good that buyers in a market would choose to purchase at a given price.

_____ 6. "As the price of a good increases, the quantity demanded decreases."

_____ 7. A list showing the quantities of a good that consumers would choose to purchase at different prices, with all other variables held constant.

_____ 8. A line showing the quantity of a good or service demanded at various prices, with all other variables held constant.

_____ 9. A movement along a demand curve in response to a change in price.

_____ 10. A shift of a demand curve in response to a change in some variable other than price.

_____ 11. The amount that a person or firm earns over a particular period.

_____ 12. The total value of everything a person or firm owns at a point in time, minus the total value of everything owed.

_____ 13. A good that people demand more of as their incomes rise.

_____ 14. A good that people demand less of as their incomes rise.

_____ 15. A good that can be used in place of some other good and that fulfills more or less the same purpose.

_____ 16. A good that is used together with some other good.

_____ 17. The set of methods a firm can use to turn inputs into outputs.

_____ 18. The amount of a good or service an individual firm would choose to produce and sell at a given price.

_____ 19. The total amount of a good or service that sellers in a market would choose to produce and sell at a given price.

_____ 20. "As the price of a good increases, the quantity supplied increases."

_____ 21. A list showing the quantities of a good or service that firms would choose to produce and sell at different prices, with all other variables held constant.

_____ 22. A line showing the quantity of a good or service supplied at various prices, with all other variables held constant.

_____ 23. A movement along a supply curve in response to a change in price.

_____ 24. A shift of a supply curve in response to some variable other than price.

_____ 25. Another good that a firm could produce using some of the same inputs as the good in question.

_____ 26. A situation that, once achieved, will not change unless some external factor, previously held constant, changes.

_____ 27. At a given price, the excess of quantity demanded over quantity supplied.

_____ 28. At a given price, the excess of quantity supplied over quantity demanded.

Word Bank

aggregation	income
alternate good	individual's quantity demanded
change in demand	inferior good
change in quantity demanded	law of demand
change in quantity supplied	law of supply
change in supply	normal good
complement	perfectly competitive market
(market) demand curve	market quantity demanded
demand schedule	market quantity supplied
equilibrium	substitute
excess demand	supply curve
excess supply	supply schedule
firm's quantity supplied	technology
imperfectly competitive market	wealth

CHAPTER HIGHLIGHTS

Fill in the blanks with the appropriate words or phrases. If you have difficulty, review the chapter and then try again.

1. A _____ is a group of buyers and sellers with the potential to trade.

2. In defining a market, we must choose the geographic area in which _____ and _____ are located. The geographic area we choose depends on the specific question we are trying to answer.

3. In _____ markets, individual buyers and sellers have some influence over the price of the product.

4. In _____ markets, each buyer and seller treats the _____ as given.

5. Supply and demand explain how prices are determined in _____ markets.

6. The individual's quantity _____ of any good is the amount that an individual would choose to buy at a particular _____.

7. The _____ of any good is the total amount that all buyers in a market would choose to purchase at a given _____.

8. The _____ of demand states that when the price of a good rises, and everything else remains the same, the quantity of the good demanded will _____.

9. The _____ shows the relationship between the price of a good and the quantity demanded, holding constant all other variables that affect demand. Each point on the curve shows the quantity that buyers would choose to buy at a specific _____.

10. The law of demand tells us that demand curves slope _____.

11. A change in a good's price causes us to *move along* the demand curve. We call this a change in _____.

12. A change in any determinant of demand—except for the good's price—causes the demand curve to _____. We call this a _____.

13. The demand for most goods (normal goods) is positively related to _____ or _____. A rise in either _____ or _____ will increase demand for these goods, and shift the demand curve to the _____.

14. When the price of a substitute rises, the demand for a good will _____, shifting the demand curve to the _____.

15. A rise in the price of a complement will _____ the demand for a good, shifting the demand curve to the _____.

16. A firm's _____ is the set of methods it can use to turn _____ into _____.

17. A competitive firm faces three constraints: (1) it's production technology, (2) the _____ of its inputs, and (3) the _____ of its output.

18. A firm's quantity _____ of any good is the amount it would choose to produce and sell at a particular _____.

19. The _____ of any good is the total amount that sellers in a market would choose to produce and sell at a given price.

20. The *law of supply* states that when the price of a good rises, and everything else remains the same, the quantity of the good supplied will _____.

21. The *supply curve* shows the relationship between the _____ of a good and the quantity supplied, holding constant the values of all other variables that affect supply. Each point on the curve shows the quantity that sellers would choose to sell at a specific

_____.

22. The *law of supply* tells us that supply curves slope _____

23. A change in a good's price causes us to *move along* the supply curve. We call this a change in _____.

24. A change in any influence on supply—except for the good's price—causes the supply curve to _____. We call this a _____.

25. A rise in the price of an input will cause supply to _____, shifting the supply curve to the _____.

26. When an alternate good becomes more profitable to produce—because its price _____ or the cost of producing it _____ —the supply curve for the good in questions will shift to the _____ .

27. Cost-saving technological advances cause supply to _____, shifting the supply curve to the _____.

28. An increase in sellers' productive capacity shifts the supply curve to the

_____.

29. A rise in the expected price of a good will _____ the supply of the good, shifting the supply curve to the _____.

30. A(n) _____ is a situation that, once achieved, will not change unless something we have been holding constant changes.

31. To find the _____ price and quantity in a competitive market, draw the supply and demand curves. The _____ is the point where the two curves intersect.

32. Any change that shifts the supply curve to the _____ will increase the equilibrium price and decrease the equilibrium quantity.

33. Any change that shifts the demand curve to the _____ will cause both the equilibrium price and quantity to increase

The next four problems concern the four key steps that economists use again and again to answer questions about the economy.

34. Key Step #1—Characterize the _____: Decide which _____ best suits the problem being analyzed, and identify the decision makers (buyers and sellers) who interact in that _____.

35. Key Step #2—Identify _____ and _____: Identify the _____ that the decision makers are trying to achieve, and the _____ they face in achieving those _____.

36. Key Step #3—Find the _____: Describe the conditions necessary for _____ in the market, and a method for determining that _____.

37. Key Step #4—What Happens when Things Change: Explore how events or government policies change the market _____.

IMPORTANT CONCEPTS

Write a brief answer for each of the following items.

1. List as many distinct variables as you can that *shift* the demand curve for a good. For each variable, indicate the direction of change that causes the demand curve to shift to the *left*. Assume that the good is *normal*.

2. List as many distinct variables as you can that *shift* the supply curve for a good. For each variable, indicate the direction of change that causes the supply curve to shift to the *right*.

3. What is the key difference between a perfectly competitive market and an imperfectly competitive market?

Indicate whether each of the next two statements is true or false, and then explain briefly.

4. "Income and wealth mean basically the same thing in economics."

5. "The phrase 'change in demand' can refer either to a shift in the demand curve or a movement along the demand curve."

SKILLS AND TOOLS

For each of the following items, follow the instructions, write the correct answer in the blank, or circle the correct answer.

1. In the following demand schedule, P is the market price and Q^D is the quantity of limousine rides demanded per week by buyers in Patterson, New Jersey.

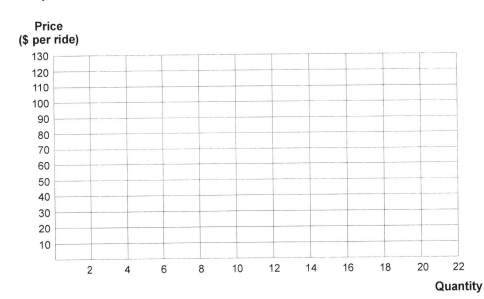

DEMAND

P	Q^D
$100	0
80	4
60	8
40	12
20	16
0	20

a. Plot the market demand curve for limousine rides. Label this curve D.

b. From this demand curve, we can see that when the market price is $50, the quantity of limousine rides demanded will be _____. If the market price rises to $90, however, the quantity demanded will (rise/fall) to _____ units per week. However, if the market price falls as low as $10, the quantity demanded will (rise/fall) to _____ units per week.

2. In the following supply schedule, P is the market price of limousine rides and Q is the quantity of rides supplied per week by sellers in Patterson, New Jersey.

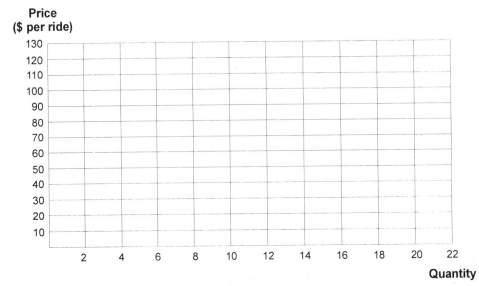

SUPPLY

P	Q^S
$ 20	0
40	4
60	8
80	12
100	16
120	20

a. Plot the market supply curve for limousine rides in the space provided. Label this curve S.

b. From this supply curve, we can see that when the market price is $50, the quantity of rides supplied will be _____. If the market price rises to $90, however, the quantity supplied will (rise/fall) to _____ units per week. However, if the market price falls as low as $30, the quantity supplied will (rise/fall) to _____ units per week.

3. In the space below, re-plot the demand curve and the supply curve for limousine rides using the data from the previous two questions.

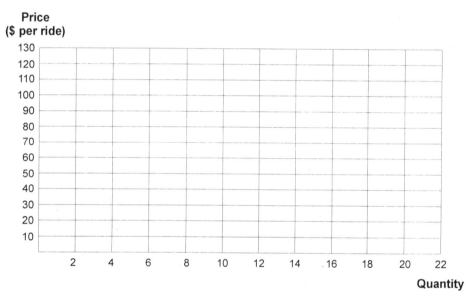

a. By examining demand and supply together, we can see that the equilibrium price in the market for limousine rides will be _____. The number of rides bought and sold per week will be _____.

b. At a price of $80 per week, there would be an excess (demand/supply) of _____ units per week in this market. Market price would tend to (rise/fall) as (buyers/sellers) compete with one another to (buy/sell) more limousine rides.

c. At a price of $40 per week, there would be an excess (demand/supply) of _____ units per week. Market price would tend to (rise/fall) as (buyers/sellers) compete with one another to (buy/sell) more limousine rides.

4. Under current conditions, the monthly demand curve and monthly supply curve for 13-inch color TVs in Golden, Colorado, are plotted below.

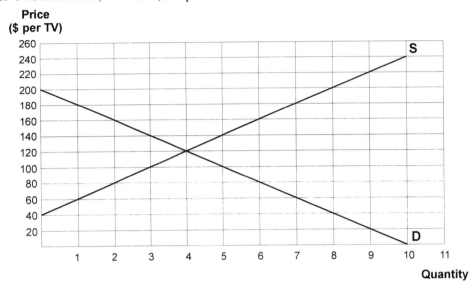

a. What is the equilibrium price of TVs? _____

b. Suppose the price of recliner chairs, a complement to TVs, falls. This will tend to (increase/decrease) the quantity of TVs demanded every month, and so shift market demand for TVs (rightward/leftward).

The table below shows data on market demand for TVs *after* the price of recliners has fallen.

P	Q^D
$200	2
160	4
120	6
80	8
40	10

c. Plot the new demand curve for TVs on the graph above.

d. What is the new equilibrium price for TVs? _____

e. Suppose the price of copper wire, an important component in the production of TVs, rises. This will tend to (increase/decrease) the quantity of TVs supplied every month, and so shift market supply of TVs (leftward/rightward).

Data on market supply of TVs after the price of copper wire has fallen are recorded in the table below.

P	Q^S
$120	2
160	4
200	6
240	8
280	10

f. Plot the new supply curve for TVs on the graph on the previous page.

g. What is the new equilibrium price for TVs after this latest change?

_____

5. Monthly data from Tuscaloosa on market demand and market supply of leather handbags have been graphed below.

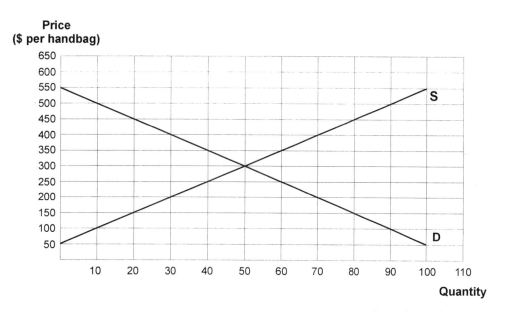

a. Complete the combined demand and supply schedules for leather handbags.

P	Q^D	Q^S
$450	_____	_____
400	_____	_____
350	_____	_____
300	_____	_____
250	_____	_____
200	_____	_____
150	_____	_____

b. If the market price were $400, quantity (demanded/supplied) would exceed quantity (demanded/supplied) and there would be an (excess demand/excess supply) equal to _____ units per period. This would cause the market price to (rise/fall) toward its equilibrium level of _____.

c. If the market price were $150, quantity (demanded/supplied) would exceed quantity (demanded/supplied) and there would be (excess demand/excess supply) equal to _____ units per period. This would cause the market price to (rise/fall) toward its equilibrium level of _____.

6. So far, we have studied market demand and market supply either as tables or as graphs. Sometimes, however, it is more convenient to express those same relationships in the form of equations. For example, suppose we know that, every week, the quantity of deep sea fishing trips buyers will demand (Q^D) is related to market price according to the equation

$$Q^D = 20 - P/15,$$

while the quantity of fishing trips supplied (Q^S) is related to market price according to the equation

$$Q^S = P/12 - 2.5.$$

Using these equations, complete the combined demand and supply schedules below. (To fill out the table, just plug market price into the demand or supply equation given above and solve for the corresponding quantity demanded or supplied.)

P	Q^D	Q^S
270	_____	_____
210	_____	_____
90	_____	_____
30	_____	_____

Now look at the table you just completed. Notice that at very low market prices, quantity demanded exceeds quantity supplied, while at higher prices quantity supplied exceeds quantity demanded. Just by looking at the data in these demand and supply schedules, we are therefore unable to determine the equilibrium price in this market.

But we *can* find the equilibrium with our equations. Suppose we let P_e stand for the unknown value of the equilibrium price in this market. While we do not know P_e, we know it is special: it is the only price at which quantity demanded will equal quantity supplied. To find P_e, we therefore simply set the equation for quantity demanded equal to the equation for quantity supplied. Setting $Q^D = Q^S$ in this way, we obtain

$$20 - P_e/15 = P_e/12 - 2.5.$$

To solve for P_e, we add 2.5 to each side, then add $P_e/15$ to each side, and get

$$22.5 = P_e/12 + P_e/15.$$

Next, putting the two terms on the righthand side over the common denominator $12 \times 15 = 180$, we obtain

$$22.5 = 27P_e/180.$$

Finally, by multiplying both sides by 180 and dividing by 27, we get the final answer

$$P_e = (22.5)(180)/27 = 150.$$

7. Using the data you generated in the preceding exercise, plot the market demand and supply curves in the space provided there. Once you've completed your graphs, locate the equilibrium market price. What is that price according to your graphs? _____ Is it the same price you obtained by solving the demand and supply equations?

_____ It should be, so if it is not, go back and see what you did wrong.)
What is the equilibrium quantity? _____ Is it the same as you would get if you plugged your answer for equilibrium price into the market demand and market supply curves? _____ (It should be.)

8. Annual market demand and market supply for tons of California cumquats are given, respectively, by the following equations

$$Q^D = 500 - P/8$$

$$Q^S = P/2 - 500.$$

Without plotting graphs for demand or supply, answer the following questions.

a. In equilibrium, the price of California cumquats will be \$_____ . The quantity of cumquats bought and sold will be _____ tons.

b. If market price were \$1,200, quantity demanded would be _____ tons and quantity supplied would be _____ tons. There would be (excess demand/excess supply) equal to _____ tons of cumquats per year.

c. If market price were $2,000, quantity demanded would be _____ tons and quantity supplied would be _____ tons. There would be (excess demand/excess supply) equal to _____ tons of cumquats per year.

15-MINUTE PRACTICE TEST

Set a timer, giving yourself just 15 minutes to answer all of the following questions. To see what you *really* know and remember, take the test at least a day *after* you've read the chapter in the text and completed the exercises in this study guide.

Multiple Choice: Circle the letter in front of the single best answer.

1. In economics, a "market" is
   a. a geographic location where buyers and sellers trade with each other.
   b. virtually always defined locally, rather than nationally or internationally.
   c. virtually always defined nationally, rather than locally or internationally.
   d. defined only *after* an exchange actually takes place.
   e. a group of buyers and sellers with the potential to trade.

2. A perfectly competitive market is one in which
   a. buyers and sellers never actually meet each other.
   b. no buyer or seller can influence the price of the product being traded.
   c. a few very large firms directly compete with each other for customers.
   d. there are no limits to the tricks sellers can play to drive their rivals out of business.
   e. all of the above.

3. Which of the following would cause a rightward shift of the demand curve in the market for eggs in St. Louis?
   a. A technological advance in the egg-producing industry
   b. An increase in the number of firms in the egg-producing industry
   c. An increase in the price of chicken feed
   d. An increase in the price of powdered eggs, a substitute for fresh eggs
   e. None of the above

4. If used books are an inferior good, then a decrease in income will cause a
   a. rightward shift of the demand curve for used books.
   b. leftward shift of the demand curve for used books.
   c. rightward shift of the supply curve for used books.
   d. leftward shift of the demand curve for used books.
   e. shift in both the demand and the supply curves for used books.

5. If the price of oranges is expected to rise, then
   a. the demand curve for oranges will shift rightward.
   b. the demand curve for oranges will shift leftward.
   c. the supply curve for oranges will shift leftward.
   d. both *a* and *c*.
   e. both *b* and *c*.

6. Which of the following would shift the supply curve for a good leftward?
   a. A rise in the price of a complement
   b. A rise in the price of an input used in producing the good
   c. A cost-saving technological advance in producing the good
   d. All of the above
   e. None of the above

7. If there is an excess supply of a good, we can generally expect
   a. the price of the good to rise.
   b. the price of the good to fall.
   c. the demand curve to shift rightward.
   d. the supply curve to shift leftward.
   e. both *c* and *d*.

8. A rise in the price of a substitute for a good will cause
   a. the equilibrium price of the good to increase and the equilibrium quantity to decrease.
   b. the equilibrium price of the good to decrease and the equilibrium quantity to increase.
   c. both the equilibrium price and the equilibrium quantity of the good to increase.
   d. both the equilibrium price and the equilibrium quantity of the good to decrease.
   e. no change in either the equilibrium price or equilibrium quantity of the good.

9. Which of the following is *not* included among the four key steps that economists use to solve problems?
   a. Identify Goals and Constraints.
   b. Graph the Equations.
   c. Find the Equilibrium.
   d. What Happens when Things Change.
   e. Characterize the Market.

10. In the market for potatoes, a rise in the price of beef (a complement) and a rise in the wage paid to farm labor (an input) would cause
    a. both the equilibrium price and equilibrium quantity to rise.
    b. both the equilibrium price and equilibrium quantity to fall.
    c. a decrease in the equilibrium quantity, and an ambiguous effect on the equilibrium price.
    d. an increase in the equilibrium price, and an ambiguous effect on the equilibrium quantity.
    e. none of the above.

True/False: For each of the following statements, circle T if the statement is true or F if the statement is false.

T   F   1. The law of demand tells us that, for most goods, a rise in income will cause an increase in quantity demanded.

T   F   2. If people want to buy more of a good at any price, sellers will want to sell more of the good, so the supply curve will shift.

T   F   3. A change in the expected future price of a good will cause both the supply curve and the demand curve for the good to shift.

T   F   4. A "change in supply" refers to a movement along the supply curve.

T   F   5. A rightward shift in the demand curve for cotton shirts will cause a rise in both the equilibrium price and equilibrium quantity of cotton shirts.

T   F   6. A rise in the price of *rayon* shirts will cause a decrease in the equilibrium price and quantity of *cotton* shirts.

T   F   7. The *first* key step of the four-step procedure is: Find the Equilibrium.

T   F   8. The *last* key step of the four-step procedure is to ask: What Happens When Things Change?

CHAPTER 4

WORKING WITH SUPPLY AND DEMAND

Fill in each blank with the appropriate words or phrases from the list provided in the word bank. (For a challenge, fill in as many blanks as you can *without* using the word bank.)

_____ 1. A government-imposed maximum price in a market.

_____ 2. The smaller of quantity supplied and quantity demanded at a particular price.

_____ 3. A market in which goods are sold illegally at a price above the legal ceiling.

_____ 4. A government-imposed maximum rent on apartments and homes.

_____ 5. A government-imposed minimum price in a market.

_____ 6. A government-imposed fee on a specific good or service.

_____ 7. The percentage change in quantity demanded caused by a 1 percent change in price.

_____ 8. A price elasticity of demand between 0 and −1.

_____ 9. A price elasticity of demand equal to 0.

_____ 10. A price elasticity of demand less than −1.

_____ 11. A price elasticity of demand approaching minus infinity.

_____ 12. A price elasticity of demand equal to −1.

_____ 13. An elasticity measured just a short time after a price change.

_____ 14. An elasticity measured a year or more after a price change.

_____ 15. The percentage change in quantity demanded caused by a 1 percent change in income.

_____ 16. A good with an income elasticity of demand between 0 and 1.

_____ 17. A good with an income elasticity of demand greater than 1.

_____ 18. The percentage change in the quantity demanded of one good caused by a 1 percent change in the price of another good.

Word Bank

black market	perfectly inelastic demand
cross-price elasticity of demand	perfectly (infinitely) elastic demand
economic luxury	price ceiling
economic necessity	price elasticity of demand
elastic demand	price floor
excise tax	rent controls
income elasticity of demand	short-run elasticity
inelastic demand	short side of the market
long-run elasticity	unitary elastic demand

CHAPTER HIGHLIGHTS

Fill in the blanks with the appropriate words or phrases. If you have difficulty, review the chapter, and then try again.

1. When quantity supplied and quantity demanded differ, the _____ of the market—whichever of the two quantities is smaller—will prevail.

2. A price _____ creates a shortage, and increases the time and trouble required to buy the good. While the price decreases, the opportunity cost may rise.

3. A price _____ creates an excess supply of a good. In order to maintain the price _____ , the government must prevent the excess supply from driving down the market price. In practice, the government often accomplishes this goal by _____ the excess supply.

4. An excise tax shifts the market _____ curve upward by the amount of the tax. For each quantity, the new higher _____ curve tells us firms' gross price, and the original, lower _____ curve tells us the _____ price.

5. An excise tax on a good causes the price paid by consumers to _____, and the price received by sellers to _____. Thus, both buyers and sellers bear part of the burden of paying the tax.

6. The price elasticity of demand (E^D) is the percentage change in _____ divided by the percentage change in _____.

7. A price elasticity of demand tells us the percentage change in quantity demanded caused by a _____ percent rise in price as we move along a demand curve from one point to another.

8. Elasticity of demand varies along a straight-line demand curve. More specifically, demand becomes more _____ as we move upward and leftward.

9. Where demand is _____, total expenditure moves in the same direction as price. Where demand is _____, total spending moves in the opposite direction as price. Finally, where demand is _____, total expenditure remains the same as price changes.

10. At any point on a demand curve, buyers' total _____ is the area of a rectangle with width equal to quantity demanded and height equal to price.

11. The more narrowly we define an item, the easier it is to find substitutes, and the _____ elastic is the demand for the good.

12. The more "necessary" we regard an item, the harder it is to find substitutes, and the _____ elastic is the demand for the good.

13. It is usual easier to find substitutes for an item in the _____ run than in the _____ run. Therefore, demand tends to be more elastic in the _____ run than in the _____ run.

14. The more of their total budgets that households spend on an item, the _____ elasticitic is demand for that item.

15. The more *elastic* the demand curve, the more of an excise tax is paid by _____. The more *inelastic* the demand curve, the more of the tax is paid by _____.

16. Income elasticity of demand is the percentage change in _____ divided by the percentage change in _____, all other influences on demand remaining constant.

17. A _____ elasticity of demand tells us the percentage change in quantity demanded of a good for each 1 percent increase in the price of some other good, all other influences on demand remaining unchanged.

IMPORTANT CONCEPTS

Write a brief answer below each of the following questions.

1.   Indicate whether the following statement is true or false, and explain briefly: "In order to affect the outcome in a market, a price floor must be set *below* the equilibrium price."

2.   List the three different types of "elasticities" discussed in Chapter 4.

a.

b.

c.

3. List two general properties of a good that tend to make demand for it more elastic.

a.

b.

4. Which type of elasticity, and what specific information about that elasticity, would enable us to conclude each of the following?

    a. A good is normal.

    b. A good is inferior.

    c. Two goods are substitutes.

    d. Two goods are complements.

    e. A good follows the law of demand.

    f. A rise in the price of the good causes total expenditure on the good to rise.

5. Suppose that from 1996 to 2000, the price of movies in a city rose an average of 12%. At the same time, the quantity of movies demanded in that city increased by 12%. Can we conclude that the price elasticity of demand for movies is equal to +1.0, and that movies therefore violate the law of demand? Explain briefly.

SKILLS AND TOOLS

1. In the space below, re-plot the demand curve and the supply curve for limousine rides using the data from questions (1) and (2) in Chapter 3, reproduced in the table below.

P	Q^D	Q^S
$100	0	16
80	4	12
60	8	8
40	12	4
20	16	0

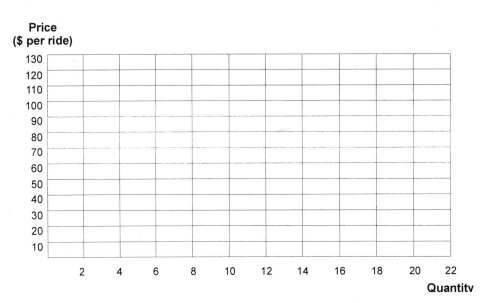

a. By examining demand and supply together, we can see that the equilibrium price in the market for limousine rides will be _____. The number of rides bought and sold per week will be _____.

b. If the government were to establish and enforce a price floor of $80 per week, there would be an excess (demand/supply) of _____ units per week in this market.

c. If the government were to establish and enforce a price ceiling of $40 per week, there would be an excess (demand/supply) of _____ units per week.

d. If the government imposed a price ceiling of $40, a black market for limousine rides would likely develop. If you tried to buy rides on the black market, you could expect to pay at least _____ per unit.

For each of the following items, follow the instructions, write the correct answer in the blank, or circle the correct answer.

Reminder: **Price elasticity of demand** measures the responsiveness of quantity demanded to price, holding constant all other influences on demand. It is found by dividing the percentage change in the quantity demanded by the percentage change in the good's price, where the base value used to calculate percentage change is the *midpoint* between the initial value and the ending value.

Thus, the formula for the percentage change in quantity demanded is:

$$\%\Delta Q^D = \frac{Q_1 - Q_0}{\frac{1}{2}(Q_1 + Q_0)}.$$

The formula for the percentage change in the price is:

$$\%\Delta P = \frac{P_1 - P_0}{\frac{1}{2}(P_1 + P_0)}.$$

Elasticity is computed by taking the ratio of these:

$$E^D = \frac{\%\Delta Q^D}{\%\Delta P}.$$

2. Calculate price elasticity over the indicated range when:

   a. Price rises from \$10 to \$14, while quantity demanded falls from 30 units to 24 units.

   _____

   b. Price declines by 20%, while quantity demanded increases 15%. _____

   c. Price rises by 12%, while quantity demanded falls from 200 units to 160 units.

   _____

   d. Quantity demanded decreases by 2% while price rises by 4%. _____

   e. Price declines from \$8 to \$6, while quantity demanded rises from 100 tons to 150 tons.

   _____

3. Upon rearranging a bit, the formula for price elasticity of demand can be reduced to the "short-cut" formula mentioned in the text:

$$E^D = \frac{Q_1 - Q_0}{Q_1 + Q_0} \times \frac{P_1 + P_0}{P_1 - P_0}$$

This formula is very useful when you are given a problem with initial and new prices and quantities. Use it to recalculate the answers to (a) and (e) in problem 1.

4. The weekly demand for new air conditioning systems in Midland, Texas, is as follows.

P	Q^D	$Q^{D'}$
1,400	0	___
1,000	12	___
600	24	___
200	36	___
0	42	___

a. Plot the demand curve. (Ignore the column of blanks for now.)

b. At a price of $1400, _____ units will be purchased each week. If the price drops to $1000, _____ units will be purchased each week. Between $1400 and $1000, the elasticity of demand for air conditioning systems is E_D = _____. Between these two prices, demand is (elastic/inelastic/unit elastic). From this we know that a decrease in price from $1400 to $1000 will (increase/decrease/have no effect on) the amount consumers spend on this good per week.

c. Between $1000 and $600, the elasticity of demand for air conditioning systems is E_D = _____. Between these two prices, demand is (elastic/inelastic/unit elastic). From this we know that a decrease in price from $1000 to $600 will (increase/decrease/ have no effect on) the amount consumers spend on this good per week.

d. Between $600 and $200, the elasticity of demand for air conditioning systems is E_D = _____. Between these two prices, demand is (elastic/inelastic/unit elastic). From this we know that a decrease in price from $600 to $200 will (increase/decrease/ have no effect on) the amount consumers spend on this good per week.

5. Now suppose that, due to a sharp rise in summer temperature, the demand for new air conditioning systems increases. In particular, at every price, consumers now demand exactly 10 more systems than they did before.

a. Fill in the column labeled $Q^{D'}$ in the table above. Graph the new demand curve and label it D′.

b. Between $1400 and $1000, the elasticity of demand for this good is now $E_{D'} =$ _____. Elasticity between these two prices has (increased/decreased/ not changed) in absolute value with the rightward shift in demand. Between $1000 and $600, the elasticity of demand for this good is now $E_{D'} =$ _____. Elasticity between these two prices has (increased/decreased/stayed unchanged) in absolute value after the rightward shift in demand. Between $600 and $200, the elasticity of demand for this product is now $E_{D'} =$ _____. Elasticity between these two prices has (increased/decreased/not changed) in absolute value after the rightward shift in demand. From the preceding, we can deduce that a rightward shift in a straight-line demand curve will always (increase/decrease/leave unchanged) the absolute value of elasticity of demand between any two prices.

6. Chapter 4 makes clear that slope and elasticity are *not* the same thing. But they *are* related. The following exercises will help you see the relationship between slope and elasticity.

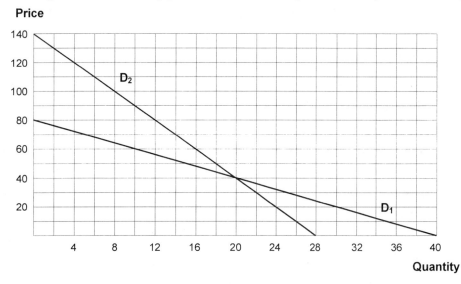

a. In the figure above, the curve labeled D_1 has a slope of _____. The curve labeled D_2 is (flatter/steeper), and it has a slope of _____. The two curves intersect where quantity demanded is _____ and price is _____ along both curves.

b. Along D_1, when price is 60, quantity demanded is _____. When price is 20, quantity demanded is _____. For a decrease in price from 60 to 20, the elasticity of demand along D_1 is $ED^1 =$ _____.

c. Along D_2, when price is 60, quantity demanded is _____. When price is 20, quantity demanded is _____. For a decrease in price from 60 to 20, the elasticity of demand along D_2 is $ED^2 =$ _____

d. Comparing answers in the previous three problems, it seems that whenever two curves share a common midpoint for the change in price and quantity demanded, the steeper curve will be more (elastic/inelastic/unit elastic) than the flatter curve over the given range.

7. **Income elasticity of demand** measures the percentage change in quantity demanded for a 1 percentage change in market income. Calculate income elasticity when

   a. Income increases from 100 to 200 and quantity demanded increases from 100 to 140.

   _____

   b. Income decreases from 200 to 180 and quantity demanded decreases from 40 to 30.

   _____

   c. Income rises by 20% and quantity demanded rises by 30%. _____

8. **Cross-price elasticity of demand** gives the percentage change in quantity demanded for a 1 percent increase in the price of some other good, all other things affecting demand held constant. Calculate the cross-price elasticity of demand for rye bread when

   a. the price of jam rises from $1 to $1.50 and the quantity of rye bread demanded decreases by 20%. _____

   b. the price of whole wheat bread falls from $1.20 to $1.00, while the quantity of rye bread demanded declines from 140 to 120. _____

9. On the supply side of the market, we can define the **price elasticity of supply** as the responsiveness of quantity supplied to changes in price. (Note: this elasticity is not covered in the chapter.) It is computed by taking the ratio of the percentage change in quantity supplied to the percentage change in price along the supply curve:

$$E^S = \frac{\%\Delta Q^S}{\%\Delta P}.$$

Once again, percentage changes are reckoned using as a base the *midpoint* between the old and new prices and quantities. Calculate the price elasticity of supply when

   a. quantity supplied rises by 10%, while price rises by 20%. _____

   b. quantity supplied increases from 1,200 to 1,800, while price rises from $13 to $17.

   _____

   c. price falls from $21 to $15, while quantity supplied declines from 360 to 280.

   _____

   d. price falls from $150 to $120, while quantity supplied does not change at all.

   _____

15-MINUTE PRACTICE TEST

Set a timer, giving yourself just 15 minutes to answer all of the following questions. To see what you *really* know and remember, take the test at least a day *after* you've read the chapter in the text and completed the exercises in this study guide.

Multiple Choice: Circle the letter in front of the single best answer.

1. Imposing a price ceiling below the equilibrium price of a good often leads to
   a. a greater supply of the good.
   b. a black market for the good.
   c. a rightward shift of the supply curve for the good.
   d. a leftward shift of the demand curve for the good.
   e. all of the above.

2. An excise tax
   a. shifts up the market supply curve.
   b. increases the price paid by buyers.
   c. decrease the (net) price received by sellers.
   d. all of the above.
   e. none of the above.

3. If the price elasticity of demand for a good is negative, we know that the good
   a. is normal.
   b. is inferior.
   c. obeys the law of demand.
   d. violates the law of demand.
   e. is inelastically demanded.

4. When the price of a good rises by 10 percent, and nothing else changes, the quantity of the good demanded falls by 5 percent. The price elasticity of demand for this good is
   a. −5%.
   b. −5.0.
   c. −2.0.
   d. 2.0.
   e. −0.5.

5. If the (absolute value of) the price elasticity of demand for a good is greater than one, then demand for the good is
   a. inelastic.
   b. elastic.
   c. inferior.
   d. normal.
   e. paranormal.

6. As we move leftward along a straight-line demand curve, the (absolute value of the) price elasticity of demand

    a. remains constant at zero.
    b. remains constant at a value of one.
    c. remains constant and equal to the (absolute value of the) slope of the demand curve.
    d. grows smaller.
    e. grows larger.

7. If a good is normal, we know that

    a. the good's price elasticity of demand is positive.
    b. demand for the good is elastic.
    c. demand for the good is inelastic.
    d. income elasticity is positive.
    e. income elasticity is negative.

8. The price elasticity of demand for a good is –2.0. When the price of this good rises,

    a. quantity demanded will rise as well.
    b. total expenditure on this good will fall.
    c. the income of those who buy the good will increase.
    d. all of the above.
    e. none of the above.

9. Which of the following would you expect to have the greatest (in absolute value) price elasticity of demand?

    a. Clothing
    b. Pants
    c. Blue jeans
    d. Levi's blue jeans
    e. All of the above would have approximately the same price elasticity of demand.

10. Among the reasons that farmers' incomes are unstable is

    a. the demand for food is elastic.
    b. the supply curve for food can shift dramatically rightward or leftward from year to year.
    c. the income elasticity for food is very high.
    d. all of the above.
    e. none of the above.

True/False: For each of the following statements, circle T if the statement is true or F if the statement is false.

T   F   1. If a price ceiling below the equilibrium price is imposed on a market, it will cause the quantity demanded to rise and the quantity supplied to fall.

T   F   2. Rent controls are one of the few examples of a price floor in market economies.

T   F   3. If the demand for mass transit in a city is inelastic, then raising fares will increase mass transit revenue.

T   F   4. The cross-price elasticity of demand between Levi's blue jeans and Wrangler's blue jeans is most likely positive.

T   F   5. If the demand for illegal drugs is inelastic, then government efforts to reduce the supply of illegal drugs are likely to cause an increase in total expenditure on them.

T   F   6. Perfectly inelastic demand occurs when the demand curve is horizontal.

T   F   7. All else being equal, the more important an item is in buyers' budgets, the more elastic is demand for the good.

T   F   8. If the demand curve for a good is a steep, straight line, then the demand for the good is inelastic at every point along that demand curve.

CHAPTER 5

CONSUMER CHOICE

Fill in each blank with the appropriate word or phrase from the list provided in the word bank. (For a challenge, fill in as many blanks as you can *without* using the word bank.)

_____ 1. The different combinations of goods a consumer can afford with a limited budget, at given prices.

_____ 2. The graphical representation of a budget constraint.

_____ 3. The price of one good relative to the price of another.

_____ 4. Pleasure or satisfaction obtained from consuming goods and services.

_____ 5. The change in total utility an individual obtains from consuming an additional unit of a good or service.

_____ 6. As consumption of a good or service increases, marginal utility decreases.

_____ 7. When a consumer can compare any two alternatives and either one is preferred, or the two are valued equally, and when the comparisons are logically consistent.

_____ 8. The process of making decisions based on their incremental, or marginal, effects.

_____ 9. A curve showing the quantity of a good or service demanded by a particular individual at each different price.

_____ 10. As the price of a good decreases, the consumer substitutes that good in place of other goods whose prices have not changed.

_____ 11. As the price of a good decreases, the consumer's purchasing power increases, causing a change in quantity demanded for the good.

Word Bank

budget constraint   marginal decision making
budget line   rational preferences
income effect   relative price
individual demand curve   substitution effect
law of diminishing marginal utility   utility
marginal utility

CHAPTER HIGHLIGHTS

Fill in the blanks with the appropriate words or phrases. If you have difficulty, review the chapter and then try again.

1. The basic principle of maximization subject to constraint tells us that economists approach problems by identifying the _____ and then determining what they are _____ and the _____ that they face.

2. A consumer's _____ identifies which combinations of goods and services the consumer can afford with a limited budget, at given prices.

3. The slope of the budget line indicates the trade-off between one good and another. If P_y is the price of the good on the vertical axis and P_x is the price of the good on the horizontal axis, then the slope of the budget line is _____.

4. A (an) _____ in income will shift the budget line upward (and rightward). A (an) _____ in income will shift the budget line downward (and leftward). These shifts are parallel—changes in income do not affect the budget line's _____.

5. When the price of a good changes, the budget line _____: both its slope and one of it intercepts will change.

6. _____ is the change in utility an individual enjoys from consuming an additional unit of a good.

7. The consumer will always choose a point on the _____, rather than a point below it.

8. The Principle of _____ states: To make the best of a situation, decision makers should consider the incremental or _____ effects of taking any action.

9. A utility-maximizing consumer will choose the point on the budget line where marginal utility _____ is the same for both goods. At that point, there is no further gain from reallocating expenditures in either direction.

10. The substitution effect of a price change arises from a change in the relative price of a good, and it always moves quantity demanded in the _____ direction of the price change. When price decreases, the substitution effect works to _____ quantity demanded; when price increases, the substitution effect works to _____ quantity demanded.

11. The _____ effect of a price change is the impact on quantity demanded that arises from a change in purchasing power over both goods.

12. For _____ goods, the substitution and the income effects work together, causing quantity demanded to move in the opposite direction of price. _____ goods, therefore, must always obey the law of _____.

13. For _____ goods, the substitution and income effects of a price change work against each other. The _____ effect moves quantity demanded in the opposite direction of the price, while the _____ effect moves it in the same direction as the price. But since the substitution effect virtually always dominates, consumption of _____ goods—like normal goods—will virtually always obey the law of _____.

14. The _____ demand curve is found by horizontally summing the individual demand curves of every consumer in the market.

15. In allocating time between two activities that provide utility, an individual will select the combination of activities such that the _____ per hour of one activity is equal to the _____ per hour of the other activity.

IMPORTANT CONCEPTS

Write a brief answer below each of the following items.

1. Briefly identify the difference between *utility* and *marginal utility*.

Indicate whether the next two statements are true or false, then explain briefly.

2. *"When we assume that consumers are rational, we essentially assume that their tastes agree with most peoples' tastes."*

3. "A consumer's tastes have nothing to do with the slope or position of his or her budget line. The consumer's tastes can change, but the budget line will remain unaffected.

4. For each of the following, indicate whether the substitution effect increases or decreases quantity demanded, and whether the income effect increases or decreases quantity demanded.

   a. The price of a normal good increases.

   b. The price of an inferior good decreases.

SKILLS AND TOOLS

For each of the following items, follow the instructions, write the correct answer in the blank, or circle the correct answer.

1. Joan has $20 to spend on novels and videos each month. Every video costs $4 to rent, and every novel costs $2 to buy. Complete the table describing different combinations of videos and novels Joan can afford.

	Videos at $4 each		Novels at $2 each	
	Quantity	Total Expenditure on Videos	Quantity	Total Expenditure on Novels
A	0	_____	10	_____
B	1	_____	8	_____
C	2	_____	6	_____
D	3	_____	4	_____
E	4	_____	2	_____
F	5	_____	0	_____

2. Using data from the previous question, plot along the horizontal axis the quantity of videos, and along the vertical axis the quantity of novels. Now plot as points each combination of videos and novels that Joan can just afford with her $20 budget each month. Label the points A through F as indicated in the table above, and connect the points with the straight line giving Joan's monthly **budget line**.

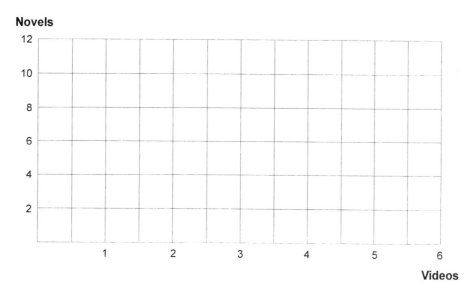

3. Jeeves is in charge of buying food and clothing for the staff at Lordly Manor. Food costs $25 per pound, and clothing costs $10 per pound. Jeeves is allowed to spend no more than $4000 per month. Alternative combinations of food and clothing Jeeves can afford within his budget are listed in the first two columns below.

Food	Clothing	B
0	400	_____
20	350	_____
40	300	_____
60	250	_____
80	200	_____
100	150	_____
120	100	_____
140	50	_____
160	0	_____

a. On the grid below, plot Jeeves' budget line using the data in the first two columns. Label the budget line "A".

b. Lord Lordly decides to increase the staff's allowance. He now gives Jeeves $5,000 to spend each month on food and clothing. In the column labeled "B" above, calculate the maximum amount of clothing Jeeves can now afford with each alternative amount of food listed in the first column. Plot Jeeves' new budget line using the data from the first and third columns. Label the new budget line "B".

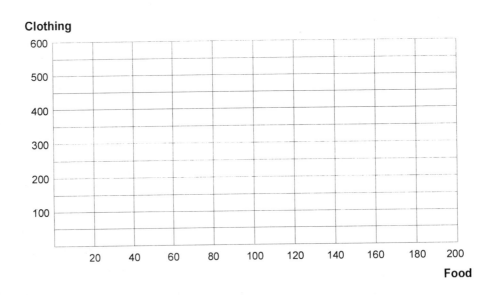

4. Carla eats only two things: artichokes and brown rice. Carla has $400 per month to spend on food. The first column below indicates different numbers of bags of rice Carla might buy.

Rice	Artichokes at $40	Artichokes at $20
400	_____	_____
320	_____	_____
240	_____	_____
160	_____	_____
80	_____	_____
0	_____	_____

a. If she pays $1 per bag of rice, and $40 per bushel of artichokes, how can Carla combine rice and artichokes in her diet? Fill in the second column of the table with the greatest number of bushels of artichokes Carla can afford given the number of bags of rice in the first column.

b. Suppose Carla moves to California where artichokes are cheap. If she still pays $1 per bag of rice, but now only pays $20 per bushel of artichokes, how can Carla now combine rice and artichokes in her diet? Fill in the third column of the table with the greatest number of bushels of artichokes Carla can now afford.

c. On the axes below, use the data in the table to plot Carla's budget lines at the two different prices for artichokes. Label with "A" the budget line when the price of artichokes is $40. Label with "B" the budget line when the price of artichokes is $20.

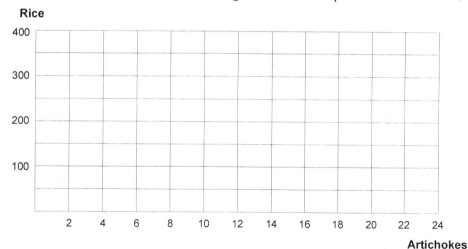

5. Marshall loves crumpets. The more he gets of them, the happier he feels. The table on page 46 shows the level of total utility Marshall enjoys when he consumes increasing numbers of crumpets per day. Compute the marginal utility Marshall enjoys from each successive pair of crumpets he consumes. Do Marshall's preferences obey the law of diminishing marginal utility? _____

Crumpets Consumed	Total Utility	Marginal Utility
0	0	
2	31	_____
4	45	_____
6	55	_____
8	63	_____
10	70	_____
12	76	_____
14	81	_____
16	85	_____
18	88	_____

6. Johnny likes both apples and oranges. Apples cost $1 each, and oranges cost $2 each. Johnny has an income of $10.

Columns 2 and 4 in the following table give the apples and oranges contained in alternative bundles A–D that Johnny can afford to buy. Columns 3 and 5 report the marginal utility Johnny derives from the last apple in the bundle and the last orange in the bundle, respectively.

Bundle	Number of Apples	Marginal Utility from Last Apple	Number of Oranges	Marginal Utility from Last Orange
A	10	3	0	—
B	8	5	1	30
C	6	10	2	20
D	4	20	3	15
E	2	35	4	10
F	0	—	5	4

a. The marginal utility *per dollar* spent on the last apple in bundle B is

_____ utils. The marginal utility *per dollar* spent on the last orange in

bundle B is _____ utils. At bundle B, the marginal utility per dollar

Johnny spends on his last orange is (greater than/equal to/less than) the marginal utility

per dollar he spends on his last apple. To maximize his utility, Johnny should buy more

(apples/oranges) and buy fewer (apples/oranges).

b. The marginal utility per dollar spent on the last orange in bundle E is
    _____ utils. The marginal utility per dollar spent on the last apple in
    bundle E is _____ utils. At bundle E, the marginal utility per dollar
    Johnny spends on his last apple is (greater than/equal to/less than) the marginal utility
    per dollar he spends on his last orange. To maximize his utility, Johnny should buy more
    (apples/oranges) and buy fewer (apples/oranges).

c. To maximize his utility, Johnny should allocate his expenditure until the marginal utility
    per dollar spent on his last orange is (greater than/equal to/less than) the marginal utility
    per dollar spent on his last apple. If he follows this rule for maximizing utility, Johnny
    will select bundle (A/B/C/D/E/F) and he will consume _____ apples
    and _____ oranges.

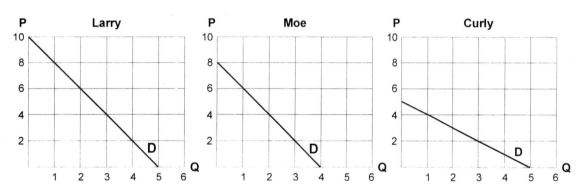

7. Larry, Moe, and Curly, whose demand curves are drawn above, are the only three buyers in
    the market for castor oil. In the table below, complete **the market demand schedule** for
    castor oil. Then plot the market demand curve on the grid provided.

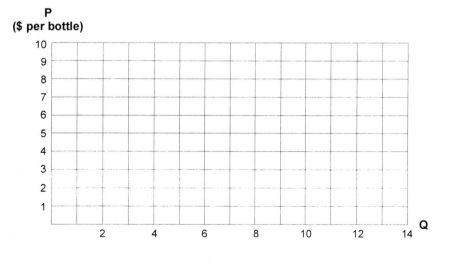

Price	Quantity Demanded
$10	_____
9	_____
8	_____
7	_____
6	_____
5	_____
4	_____
3	_____
2	_____
1	_____

15-MINUTE PRACTICE TEST

Set a timer, giving yourself just 15 minutes to answer all of the following questions. To see what you *really* know and remember, take the test at least a day *after* you've read the chapter in the text and completed the exercises in this study guide.

Multiple Choice: Circle the letter in front of the single best answer.

1. Which of the following statements about the budget line is true?
   a. The consumer can afford every combination of goods on the budget line.
   b. The consumer can afford every combination of goods below the budget line, but not those on the line.
   c. The consumer can afford only those combinations of goods along the upper-half of the budget line.
   d. The consumer can afford only those combinations of goods along the lower-half of the budget line.
   e. The budget line does not tell us anything about which combinations of goods the consumer can afford.

2. If the price of the good on the vertical axis rises, then the budget line will
   a. rotate upward, with its horizontal intercept remaining unchanged.
   b. rotate downward, with its horizontal intercept remaining unchanged.
   c. rotate upward, with its vertical intercept remaining unchanged.
   d. rotate downward, with is vertical intercept remaining unchanged.
   e. shift, with no change in its slope.

3. When the price of the good on the horizontal axis rises,
   a. the budget line becomes steeper.
   b. the budget line becomes flatter.
   c. the budget line shifts rightward, with no change in slope.
   d. the budget line shifts leftward, with no change in slope.
   e. the budget line may shift in either direction, or become steeper or flatter, depending on the consumer's tastes.

4. A rise in income will
   a. shift the budget line rightward, and increase its slope.
   b. shift the budget line leftward, and decrease its slope.
   c. shift the budget line rightward, but leave its slope unchanged.
   d. shift the budget line leftward, but leave its slope unchanged.
   e. none of the above.

5. If the law of diminishing marginal utility holds, then each time we increase the quantity of a good consumed by one unit,

    a. total utility decreases, but by less and less each time.
    b. total utility increases, but by less and less each time.
    c. total utility decreases by more and more each time.
    d. total utility increases by more and more each time.
    e. total utility first decreases and then, beyond a certain point, increases.

6. When the price of a normal good decreases,

    a. the substitution effect works to increase quantity demanded, but the income effect works to decrease quantity demanded.
    b. the substitution effect works to decrease quantity demanded, but the income effect works to increase quantity demanded.
    c. the substitution effect works to increase quantity demanded, but the income effect works to leave quantity demanded unchanged.
    d. both the substitution effect and the income effect work to increase quantity demanded.
    e. both the substitution effect and the income effect work to decrease quantity demanded.

7. Suppose that tomatoes cost $2 per pound, while apples cost $1 per pound. When someone is consuming the utility-maximizing quantities of tomatoes and apples,

    a. the total utility of tomatoes is twice the total utility of apples.
    b. the total utility of apples is twice the total utility of tomatoes.
    c. the additional utility from one more tomato would equal the additional utility from one more apple.
    d. the additional utility of one more apple would be twice the additional utility from one more tomato.
    e. the additional utility from one more tomato would be twice the additional utility from one more apple.

8. Someone who wishes to maximize total utility should consume the combination of goods for which

    a. total utility is equal for all goods.
    b. total utility per dollar is equal for all goods.
    c. marginal utility is equal for al! goods.
    d. marginal utility per dollar is equal for all goods.
    e. total utility divided by marginal utility is equal for all goods.

9. Suppose that a consumer likes both orange juice and cola, but likes cola much more. When she is consuming the optimal quantities of both drinks, we know that

    a. the marginal utility of cola is greater than that for orange juice.
    b. the marginal utility of orange juice is greater than that for cola.
    c. the marginal utility per dollar spent on cola is greater than that for orange juice.
    d. the marginal utility per dollar of orange juice is greater than that for cola.
    e. none of the above.

10. Which of the following is most likely to be an inferior good?

    a. Air travel
    b. Steak
    c. Starbucks coffee
    d. Ground beef
    e. Fresh squeezed orange juice

Questions 11 through 14 refer to the appendix to Chapter 4

11. Which of the following statements is correct?

    a. As a consumer moves rightward along an indifference curve, he is better off.
    b. A consumer prefers higher indifference curves to lower ones.
    c. The $MRS_{y,x}$ is the rate at which a consumer can substitute good y for good x along his budget line.
    d. All of the above.
    e. None of the above.

12. The optimal combinations of goods x and y will satisfy the condition that:

    a. $p_x / p_y = p_y / p_x$
    b. $MRS_{y,x} = p_x / p_y$
    c. $MRS_{y,x} = p_x \cdot p_y$
    d. $MRS_{y,x} = p_x$
    e. $MRS_{y,x} = p_y$

13. As we move leftward along an indifference curve (with good y on the vertical axis and good x on the horizontal axis),

    a. the consumer is made worse off.
    b. the consumer's income decreases.
    c. $MRS_{y,x}$ increases.
    d. the ratio p_y / p_x decreases.
    e. the ratio p_x / p_y decreases.

14. If burgers cost $3 each and bananas cost $1 each, then an individual is consuming the optimal combination of these two goods when

    a. the quantities of burgers and bananas are equal.
    b. the quantity of bananas is 3 times the quantity of burgers.
    c. the quantity of burgers is 3 times the quantity of bananas.
    d. the individual could trade 1 burger for 3 bananas and remain indifferent.
    e. the individual could trade 1 banana for 3 burgers and remain indifferent.

True/False: For each of the following statements, circle T if the statement is true or F if the statement is false.

T   F   1. When good Y is plotted on the vertical axis, and good X is plotted on the horizontal axis, then the slope of the budget line will equal the negative of the price of good Y divided by the price of good X.

T   F   2. A consumer who likes odd combinations of goods—like ice cream with ketchup or maple syrup on spaghetti—would be considered "irrational" by economists.

T   F   3. A consumer can afford to buy all combinations of goods on or below the budget line.

T   F   4. When the price of an inferior good decreases, both the substitution effect and the income effect work to increase quantity demanded.

T   F   5. The substitution effect always works to move quantity demanded in the opposite direction of a price change.

T   F   6. Consumers who judge quality by price, as with jewelry or designer clothing, would be considered "irrational" by economists.

T   F   7. When instruction in one subject becomes more effective, a rational student will always choose to score higher on tests in that subject.

T   F   8. The market demand curve is found by vertically summing all the individual demand curves in the market.

CHAPTER 6

PRODUCTION AND COST

Fill in each blank with the appropriate word or phrase from the list provided in the word bank. (For a challenge, fill in as many blanks as you can *without* using the word bank.)

_____ 1. An organization owned and operated by private individuals, that specializes in production.

_____ 2. Total revenue minus total cost.

_____ 3. A firm owned by a single individual.

_____ 4. A firm owned and usually operated by several individuals.

_____ 5. A firm owned by those who buy shares of stock and whose liability is limited to the amount of their investment in the firm.

_____ 6. The time costs and other costs required to carry out market exchanges.

_____ 7. The process of reducing risk by spreading sources of income among different alternatives.

_____ 8. A method by which inputs are combined to produce a good or service.

_____ 9. Tell us the maximum amount of output a firm can produce over some period of time from each combination of inputs.

_____ 10. A time horizon long enough for a firm to vary all of its inputs.

_____ 11. A time horizon during which at least one of the firm's inputs cannot be varied.

_____ 12. An input whose quantity remains constant, regardless of how much output is produced.

_____ 13. An input whose usage changes as the level of output changes.

_____ 14. The maximum quantity of output that can be produced from a given combination of inputs.

_____ 15. The additional output produced when one more worker is hired.

_____ 16. The marginal product of labor increases as more labor is hired.

_____ 17. The marginal product of labor decreases as more labor is hired.

_____ 18. As more and more of any input is added to a fixed amount of other inputs, its marginal product will eventually decline.

_____ 19. A cost that was incurred in the past and which does not change in response to a present decision.

_____ 20. Money actually paid out for the use of inputs.

_____ 21. The cost of inputs for which there is no direct money payment.

_____ 22. Costs of fixed inputs.

_____ 23. Costs of variable inputs.

_____ 24. The cost of *all* inputs that are fixed in the short run.

_____ 25. The cost of *all* variable inputs used in producing a particular level of output.

_____ 26. The costs of *all* inputs—fixed and variable.

_____ 27. Total fixed cost divided by the quantity of output produced.

_____ 28. Total variable cost divided by the quantity of output produced.

_____ 29. Total cost divided by the quantity of output produced.

_____ 30. The increase in total cost from producing one more unit of output.

_____ 31. The cost of producing each quantity of output when the least-cost input mix is chosen in the long run.

_____ 32. The cost per unit of output in the long run, when all inputs are variable.

_____ 33. The collection of fixed inputs at a firm's disposal.

_____ 34. When long-run average total cost decreases as output increases.

_____ 35. When long-run average total cost increases as output increases.

_____ 36. When long-run average total cost is unchanged as output. increases.

Word Bank

average fixed cost	long-run total cost
average total cost	marginal cost
average variable cost	marginal product of labor
business firm	partnership
constant returns to scale	plant
corporation	production function
diminishing marginal returns to labor	profit
diseconomies of scale	short run
diversification	sole proprietorship
economies of scale	sunk costs
explicit costs	technology
fixed costs	transaction costs
fixed input	total cost
implicit costs	total fixed cost
increasing marginal returns to labor	total product
law of diminishing marginal returns	total variable cost
long run	variable costs
long-run average total cost	variable input

CHAPTER HIGHLIGHTS

Fill in the blanks with the appropriate words or phrases. If you have difficulty, review the chapter and then try again.

1. Production is the process of combining _____ to make

   _____ .

2. For each different combination of inputs, the tells us the _____ tells us the maximum quantity of output a firm can produce over some period of time.

3. The _____ is a time horizon during which at least one of the firm's inputs cannot be varied.

4. _____ are those whose quantity remains constant, regardless of how much output is produced. _____ are those whose quantity changes as the level of output changes.

5. Total Product is the _____ quantity of output that can be produced from any given combination of _____.

6. The marginal product of labor (MPL) is the _____ produced when _____ is hired.

7. The law of _____ (marginal) returns states that as we continue to add more of any one input (holding the other inputs constant), its _____ will eventually decline.

8. A firm's total cost of production is the _____ of the owners—everything they must give up in order to produce output.

9. A sunk cost is a cost that was paid in the past and will not change regardless of a present decision. Sunk costs should be _____ when making current decisions.

10. Marginal Cost (MC) is the increase in _____ from producing one more unit of output.

11. When the marginal product of labor (MPL) rises, MC _____; when MPL falls, MC _____. Since MPL ordinarily rises and then falls, MC will ordinarily _____ and then _____. That is, the _____ curve is U-shaped.

12. At low levels of output, the MC curve lies below the _____ and _____ curves, so these curves will slope downward.

13. At higher levels of output, the MC curve will rise above the _____ and _____ curves.

14. The MC curve intersects the _____ points of the AVC and ATC curves.

15. In the long run, there are no _____ inputs or _____ costs; all inputs and all costs are _____. The firm must decide what *combination* of inputs to use in producing any level of output.

16. In the long run, to produce any given level of output, the firm will choose the input mix with the _____ cost.

17. Long-run total cost can be _____ than or equal to, but never _____ than short-run total cost. The same is true of long run *average* total cost: it can be _____ than or equal to short run average total cost (ATC), but never _____ than ATC.

18. In the _____, a firm can only move along its current ATC curve. In the _____, however, it can move from one ATC curve to another, by varying the size of its plant. As it does so, it will also be moving along its _____ curve.

19. When _____ rises proportionately less than output, production is characterized by economies of scale, and the _____ curve slopes downward.

20. When _____ rises more than in proportion to output, there are diseconomies of scale, and the _____ curve slopes upward.

21. When both _____ and _____ rise by the same proportion, production is characterized by constant returns to scale, and the _____ curve is _____.

IMPORTANT CONCEPTS

Write a brief answer below each of the following items.

1. List three advantages of production by firms with employees rather than production by independent contractors.

    a.

    b.

    c.

2. From the firm's point of view, what is the key difference between the short run and the long run?

3. Briefly state the difference between each of the following pairs of terms.

    a. total product vs. marginal product of labor

    b. increasing returns to labor vs. diminishing returns to labor

    c. average total cost vs. long-run average total cost

    d. economies of scale vs. diseconomies of scale

    e. diseconomies of scale vs. diminishing returns to labor

4. Identify each of the following (use abbreviations, e.g. "TC" for total cost):

   a. $\Delta Q/\Delta L$ = _____

   b. TFC/Q = _____

   c. TVC/Q = _____

   d. TFC + TVC = _____

   e. ATC – AFC = _____

   f. $\Delta TC/\Delta Q$ = _____

   g. LRTC /Q = _____

SKILLS AND TOOLS

For each of the following items, follow the instructions, write the correct answer in the blank, or circle the correct answer.

1. Golden Acres wheat farm can produce different amounts of wheat per season depending on the amount of labor it uses. The following is the farm's total product (TP) for different numbers of workers employed.

Number of Workers	TP	MPL
0	0	
1	100	____
2	300	____
3	700	____
4	1,000	____
5	1,200	____
6	1,300	____
7	1,350	____

Total Product

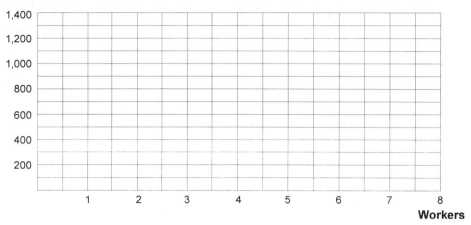

MPL

a. In the topmost grid, plot Golden Acres' total product curve.

b. Calculate the farm's marginal product of labor (MPL) for each one-worker increase in employment. Enter your calculations in the table.

c. Plot the firm's MPL curve on the lower grid. Since MPL refers to a *change* in employment, be sure to plot it *betweeen* the levels of employment for which you calculate it.

d. Looking at this graph, we can see that production of wheat at Golden Acres (does/ does not) obey the law of diminishing marginal returns. The marginal product of labor is (always positive/sometimes negative), and as more workers are hired it (stays constant/ declines/increases).

2. Golden Acres, the farm from the previous question, has fixed costs of $20,000 per season. It can hire workers for $2,000 per season each. Complete the following table of Golden Acres' costs.

Number of Workers	TP	TFC $	TVC $	TC $	AFC $	AVC $	ATC $	MC $
0	0	___	___	___	___	___	___	
1	100	___	___	___	___	___	___	___
2	300	___	___	___	___	___	___	___
3	700	___	___	___	___	___	___	___
4	1000	___	___	___	___	___	___	___
5	1200	___	___	___	___	___	___	___
6	1300	___	___	___	___	___	___	___
7	1350	___	___	___	___	___	___	___

3. Using data from the previous question, plot ATC and MC curves for Golden Acres on the grid below. (Don't bother to plot ATC at output of 100 or 300 and remember to plot MC at the midpoint of the range over which you compute it.)

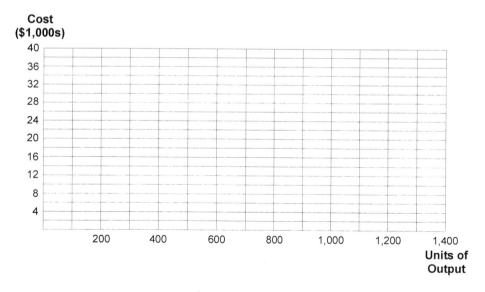

4. Blaze Busters, a producer of chemical fire retardant, had its records destroyed in a fire last week. Help the owners get back on their feet by reconstructing their cost data from these fragments they managed to save.

Weekly Output	TFC	TVC	TC	AFC	AVC	ATC	MC
0	$100	$0	____	– – –	– – –	– – –	
1	____	150	____	____	____	____	____
2	____	280	____	____	____	____	____
3	____	380	____	33.3	____	____	____
4	____	____	$ 500	____	100	____	____
5	____	____	630	____	____	126	____
6	____	____	760	____	____	____	____
7	____	____	1,010	____	____	____	250
8	____	____	1,700	____	____	____	____

5. Leo Knell produces electric trains, and his weekly cost curves are drawn below. Leo knows his trains, but he can't read graphs very well. Let's help him out.

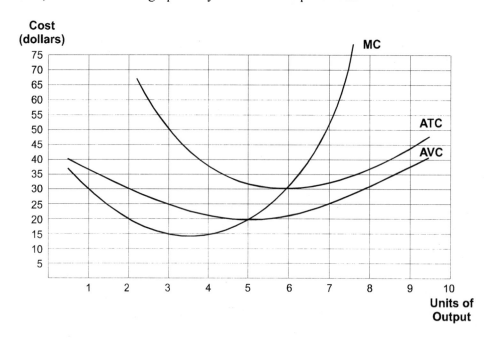

a. At output of three trains per week, average total cost is _____ and
    average variable cost is_____. At output of seven trains per week,
    average total cost is _____; average variable cost is
    _____. Over the range from three to seven trains, marginal cost is
    (increasing/constant/decreasing).

b. Average variable cost achieves its minimum value of _____ when
    output is _____ trains. Average total cost achieves its minimum value
    when output is _____ trains.

c. If Leo wants his average total cost to be $50, he should produce _____
    trains per week. If he wants his marginal cost to be $45 he should produce an output of
    _____ trains per week. Marginal cost and average total cost are equal
    to each other when output is _____ trains. Marginal cost and average
    variable cost are equal to each other when output is _____ trains.

d. Because ATC = AVC + AFC, we know that average fixed cost will be equal to (choose
    one: AVC + ATC or ATC × AVC or ATC – AVC). On the graph on page 62, this means
    that average fixed cost can be read as the (vertical distance/horizontal distance) between
    the (ATC curve and the AVC curve/MC curve and the ATC curve/MC curve and the
    AVC curve). For instance, at an output of five trains per week, average fixed cost is
    _____; at an output of 7 trains per week, average fixed cost is
    _____.

6. ***What's Wrong with This Picture?*** Find four things wrong in the graph below.

    a. _____.

    b. _____.

    c. _____.

    d. _____.

15-MINUTE PRACTICE TEST

Set a timer, giving yourself just 15 minutes to answer all of the following questions. To see what you *really* know and remember, take the test at least a day *after* you've read the chapter in the text and completed the exercises in this study guide.

Multiple Choice: Circle the letter in front of the single, best answer.

1. A partnership is defined as
   a. any firm that is owned by either two or fewer private individuals.
   b. the same as a corporation.
   c. any business firm owned by professionals, e.g. lawyers or doctors.
   d. a business firm that is co-owned by private individuals and government agencies.
   e. none of the above.

2. A plywood firm uses three inputs—labor, lumber, and saws. Although it can vary its labor each week, it must order its lumber six months in advance. Further, it would take the firm a year to sell its saws, or acquire new saws. For this firm, the long run is
   a. any time period longer than one week.
   b. any time period longer than one week and shorter than six months.
   c. any time period longer than six months.
   d. any time period longer than six months and shorter than one year.
   e. any time period longer than one year.

3. When a firm increases its employment from four to five workers, with no other change, its total output rises from 1,000 to 1,500. For this change in employment, the marginal product of labor is
   a. 100.
   b. 200.
   c. 250.
   d. 300.
   e. 500.

4. If the MPL rises over a particular range of output, then—over that range—
   a. MC rises.
   b. MC falls.
   c. ATC rises.
   d. ATC falls.
   e. both MC and ATC rise.

5. Whenever the marginal cost curve lies above the average total cost curve, an increase in output will cause
   a. the marginal cost curve to shift upward.
   b. the marginal cost curve to shift downward.
   c. the average total cost curve to shift upward.
   d. the average total cost curve to shift downward.
   e. none of the above.

6. Which of the following is an example of an implicit cost to a farmer?

   a. The wages and salaries of the farm's workers
   b. The rent that the farmer pays to a landowner
   c. The interest the farmer must pay on bank loans
   d. The monthly costs of seeds, fertilizer, and other raw materials
   e. None of the above

7. In the short run, as output rises, the distance between the firm's TC and TVC curve

   a. increases.
   b. remains constant.
   c. decreases.
   d. first increases, then decreases.
   e. first decreases, then increases.

8. Which of the following might describe the behavior of a firm's costs in the *short run*?

   a. Economies of scale
   b. Diseconomies of scale
   c. Constant returns to scale
   d. All of the above
   e. None of the above

9. The firm's marginal cost curve

   a. intersects the minimum point of the ATC curve only.
   b. intersects the minimum point of the AVC curve only.
   c. intersects the minimum point of both the AVC and ATC curve.
   d. intersects the maximum point of both the AVC and ATC curve.
   e. none of the above.

10. If a firm doubles its output, but finds that its LRTC *less than doubles*, the firm is experiencing

    a. economies of scale.
    b. constant returns to scale.
    c. diseconomies of scale.
    d. increasing returns to labor.
    e. diminishing returns to labor.

True/False: For each of the following statements, circle T if the statement is true or F if the statement is false.

T   F   1. The three major types of business firms are: sole proprietorship, public agency, and partnership.

T   F   2. The law of diminishing (marginal) returns tells us that as the firm increases its output by varying all of its inputs together, the average cost of production will rise.

T   F   3. In making a decision, all costs—whether sunk or not—should be considered.

T   F   4. The *long run* for a business firm is a time period during which at least one of its inputs is variable.

T   F   5. The *short run* for a business firm is a time period during which at least one of its inputs is variable.

T   F   6. At any level of output, a firm's ATC can be greater than or equal to, but not less than, its LRATC.

T   F   7. As output increases in the short run, average fixed cost always declines.

T   F   8. As output rises in the short run, ATC always rises.

Numerical Word Problem: An ice manufacturer produces ice blocks using just two inputs that it must pay for: freezers and labor. The freezers each cost $200 per month in foregone interest and maintenance. Workers are paid $2,000 per month. The firm currently has 5 freezers. With three workers, the firm can produce 1,000 ice blocks per month. With four workers, it can produce 1,200 ice blocks per month.

Calculate each of the following:

1. TC with 3 workers = _____;
   TC with 4 workers = _____

2. TFC with 3 workers = _____;
   TFC with 4 workers = _____

3. TVC with 3 workers = _____;
   TVC with 4 workers = _____

4. ATC with 3 workers = _____;
   ATC with 4 workers = _____

5. AFC with 3 workers = _____;
   AFC with 4 workers = _____

6. AVC with 3 workers = _____;
   AVC with 4 workers = _____

7. MPL when labor increases from 3 to 4 workers = _____

8. MC when labor increases from 3 to 4 workers = _____

CHAPTER 7

HOW FIRMS MAKE DECISIONS: PROFIT MAXIMIZATION

Fill in each blank with the appropriate word or phrase from the list provided in the word bank. (For a challenge, fill in as many blanks as you can *without* using the word bank.)

_____ 1. Total revenue minus accounting costs.

_____ 2. Total revenue minus all costs of production, explicit and implicit.

_____ 3. A curve that indicates, for different prices, the quantity of output that customers will purchase from a particular firm.

_____ 4. The total inflow of receipts from selling a given amount of output.

_____ 5. A negative profit, when total cost exceeds total revenue.

_____ 6. The change in total revenue from producing one more unit of output.

_____ 7. A firm maximizes its profit by taking any action that adds more to its revenue than to its cost.

_____ 8. A firm should continue to produce in the short run if total revenue exceeds total variable costs; otherwise, it should stop producing in the short run.

_____ 9. A permanent cessation of production when a firm leaves an industry.

_____ 10. A person or group that hires someone to do a job.

_____ 11. A person hired to do a job.

_____ 12. The situation that arises when an agent has interests that conflict with the principal's, and has the ability to pursue those interests.

_____ 13. When owners, dissatisfied with the profits they are earning, replace the firm's management team.

_____ 14. When outsiders buy up a firm's shares with the goal of replacing the management team and increasing profits.

_____ 15. When a firm's management arranges a takeover by another firm deemed unlikely to fire them.

_____ 16. A firm that undertakes a friendly takeover.

_____ 17. Rights to purchase shares of stock at a prespecified price.

Word Bank

accounting profit	marginal revenue (MR)
agent	principal
demand curve facing the firm	principal-agent problem
economic profit	shutdown rule
exit	stock options
friendly takeover	stockholder revolt
hostile takeover	total revenue
loss	white knight
marginal approach to profit	

CHAPTER HIGHLIGHTS

Fill in each blank with the appropriate word or phrase. If you have difficulty, review the chapter and then try again.

1. The firm is viewed as a single economic decision maker, whose goal is to _____ its owners' _____.

2. The proper measure of profit for understanding and predicting the behavior of firms is _____ profit. Unlike _____ profit, _____ profit recognizes all costs of production—both explicit and implicit.

3. The _____ facing the firm tells us, for different prices, the quantity of output that customers will choose to purchase from the firm.

4. The _____ facing the firm also shows us the maximum price the firm can charge to sell any given amount of output.

5. For any level of output the firm might want to produce, it must pay the cost of the
   _____ method of production. This is the firm's _____
   constraint.

6. The firm faces constraints that limit its choices of revenue and costs. For each level of
   output the firm might choose, its _____ determines the price it can charge
   and the total revenue it will receive. Its production _____ and the prices
   of its input determine the total cost it must bear.

7. In the total revenue-total cost approach, the firm calculates profit = TR − TC at each
   _____ and selects the _____ where
   _____ is greatest.

8. Marginal revenue (MR) is the change in total revenue from producing
   _____. Mathematically, MR is calculated by dividing the change in
   _____ by the change in _____, or, using symbols,
   MR = _____.

9. When a firm faces a downward-sloping demand curve, each increase in output causes a
   revenue gain—from selling additional output at the new price—and a revenue loss—from
   having to lower the price on all previous units of output. Marginal revenue is therefore
   _____ than the price of the last unit of output.

10. An increase in output will always raise profit as long as _____ is greater
    than _____. An increase in output will always lower profit whenever
    _____ is less than _____.

11. The firm should increase output whenever marginal revenue is _____
    than marginal cost, and lower output when marginal revenue is _____
    than marginal cost.

12. To maximize profit, the firm should produce the quantity of output where the vertical
    distance between the _____ and _____ curves is
    greatest, and the _____ curve lies above the _____
    curve.

13. To maximize profit, the firm should produce the level of output closest to the point where
    _____ equals _____, that is, the level of output at
    which the _____ and _____ curves intersect.

14. The marginal approach to profit states that a firm should take any actin that adds more to its
    _____ than to its _____.

15. Let Q^* be the output level at which MR = MC. Then, in the short run, if total revenue is greater than _____ at Q^*, the firm should keep producing. If total revenue is less than _____ at Q^*, the firm should shut down.

16. A firm should _____ in the long run when—at its best possible output level—it has any size loss at all.

17. A _____ is a person or group who hires someone to do a job. An _____ is the person hired to do that job.

18. The _____ problem arises when an agent has (1) interests that conflict with the _____ and (2) the ability to pursue those interests.

IMPORTANT CONCEPTS

Write a brief answer below each of the following questions.

1. What are the two definitions of profit? Give a simple equation that expresses each definition.

   a.

   b.

2. Are marginal revenue and total revenue the same? If not, what is the difference between them? If so, why do economists use two different terms to describe the same thing?

3. Suppose the marginal revenue curve crosses the marginal cost curve at *two* points. How can we tell which point is the profit-maximizing output level?

4. State the rule that tells us (a) when a firm should stay open in the short run; (b) when a firm should shut down in the short run.

5. What is the key difference between a hostile takeover and a friendly takeover?

SKILLS AND TOOLS

For each of the following items, follow the instructions, write the correct answer in the blank, or circle the correct answer.

1. Last summer, Paula hired an economics student from Big U. to determine the demand curve facing her firm, Paula's Pickled Peppers. The student presented Paula with the demand curve in the figure below. Data on the horizontal axis are pecks of peppers per period. The vertical axis measures price in dollars.

   a. Complete the following table using information from the demand curve.

Price	Output	Total Revenue
$10	_____	_____
9	_____	_____
8	_____	_____
7	_____	_____
6	_____	_____
5	_____	_____
4	_____	_____
3	_____	_____
2	_____	_____
1	_____	_____
0	_____	_____

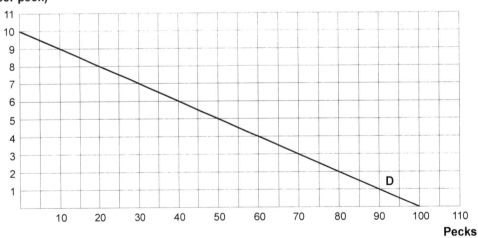

b. On the grid provided, plot the total revenue (TR) curve for Paula's Pickled Peppers.

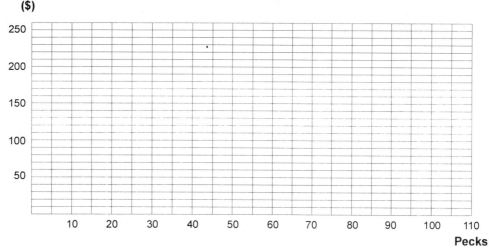

c. If Paula wants to maximize her revenue from selling peppers, how many pecks of peppers should she push each period? _____ What price should she charge? _____ How much revenue will she earn?

_____

2. Paula may not be perfect, but she is nobody's patsy. She knows that revenue is only half of the story in business. What she cares *most* about is profit. After all, profit is what she gets to keep for herself, and she picked this particular profession for one reason only—its potential pecuniary rewards. Paula's peppers cost her $4 per peck to pick and pack. She has no fixed costs, so her total costs are given by the equation

$$TC = \$4q$$

where q is the number of pecks of peppers produced.

a. Carefully plot Paula's total cost curve on the grid provided in part (b) of the previous question. You will now have Paula's TR and TC curves on the same graph.

b. Reading from those two graphs, we can see that when Paula produces:

an output of 10 her profit will be _____

an output of 20 her profit will be _____

an output of 30 her profit will be _____

an output of 40 her profit will be _____

an output of 50 her profit will be _____

an output of 60 her profit will be _____

c. From the graph, we can see that if Paula wants to maximize her profit, she should produce an output of _____ pecks per period. From the demand curve in problem (1), this will mean Paula must charge a price of _____. Paula will then earn total revenue of _____ per period. Her total cost will be _____. That will leave Paula with a profit of _____ per period.

3. The following data on total revenue and total cost have been reported by your Vice President for Planning.

Output	Total Revenue	Marginal Revenue	Total Cost	Marginal Cost
0	$ 0		$50	
1	50	_____	60	_____
2	90	_____	75	_____
3	120	_____	95	_____
4	140	_____	120	_____
5	150	_____	150	_____
6	150	_____	185	_____

a. Your VP does not know how to compute marginal revenue and marginal cost, so you will have to fill in the table yourself.

b. In trying to decide how much to produce, you first compare MR and MC for the change from zero to one unit of output. Because you find that (MR>MC / MR=MC / MR<MC) you decide that you (should/should not) make that change because doing so adds (less/the same/more) to the firm's total revenue than it does to the firm's total cost.

c. Next you compare MR and MC for the move from 1 to 2 units of output. Because you find that (MR>MC / MR=MC / MR<MC) you decide that you (should/should not) make that move because doing so adds (less/more) to the firm's total revenue than it does to the firm's total cost.

d. Then you compare MR and MC for the move from 2 to 3 units of output. Because you find that (MR>MC / MR=MC / MR<MC) you decide that you (should/should not) make that move because doing so adds (less/more) to the firm's total revenue than it does to the firm's total cost.

e. Now you compare MR and MC for the move from 3 to 4 units of output. Because you find that (MR>MC / MR=MC / MR<MC) you decide that you (should/should not) make

that move because doing so adds (less/more) to the firm's total revenue than it does to the firm's total cost.

f. Next you compare MR and MC for the move from 4 to 5 units of output. Because you find that (MR>MC / MR=MC / MR<MC) you decide that you (should/should not) make that move because doing so adds (less/more) to the firm's total revenue than it does to the firm's total cost.

g. Finally you compare MR and MC for the move from 5 to 6 units of output. Because you find that (MR>MC / MR=MC / MR<MC) you decide that you (should/should not) make that move because doing so adds (less/more) to the firm's total revenue than it does to the firm's total cost.

h. Having completed your analysis, you decide that in order to maximize profit you should produce _____ units of output. By doing so, you earn profit of _____. You can tell that you've chosen the best output, because had you decided to produce one unit less than that, your profit would have been _____; while if you had decided to produce one unit more than that your profit would have been _____.

4. Paula, who already produces pickled peppers, decides she'd like to branch into peaches, too. Her new venture, Paula's Prime Peaches, faces the following demand schedule

Quantity Demanded	Price	TR	MR
1	$28	_____	
2	26	_____	_____
3	24	_____	_____
4	22	_____	_____
5	20	_____	_____
6	18	_____	_____
7	16	_____	_____
8	14	_____	_____
9	12	_____	_____
10	10	_____	_____

a. Complete the table.

b. If the marginal cost to Paula of each bushel of peaches is a constant $10, how many peaches should Paula pick and package in order to maximize her profit?

_____

c. If the weather is good, the marginal cost of picking and packing peaches falls to $6 per bushel. If she gets good weather, how many peaches should Paula pick and pack in order to maximize her profit? _____

d. If the weather is good, and some of her neighbors help out for free, the marginal cost of picking and packing peaches will fall to $2 per bushel. If her neighbors help her out and the weather is good, how many peaches should Paula pick and pack?

_____

5. Roger bought a Bed & Breakfast Inn (B & B) in Annapolis, Maryland. It's a good location, but he borrowed heavily to bankroll the business. Mortgage interest, interest on his renovation loan, taxes insurance and other fixed charges total $11,200 per month. At $150 per night, Roger's eight rooms can yield revenue of $33,600 per month, assuming 100% occupancy. Roger contracts out for cleaning, cooking and waitstaff at $4,200 per month. These contracts are for one month's service, and can be renewed each month if Roger chooses to do so. He therefore considers these latter expenses variable from month to month.

Month	Occupancy Rate	TR	TVC	TFC	Profit
January	10%	_____	_____	_____	_____
February	10%	_____	_____	_____	_____
March	20%	_____	_____	_____	_____
April	25%	_____	_____	_____	_____
May	60%	_____	_____	_____	_____
June	85%	_____	_____	_____	_____
July	95%	_____	_____	_____	_____
August	95%	_____	_____	_____	_____
September	80%	_____	_____	_____	_____
October	50%	_____	_____	_____	_____
November	20%	_____	_____	_____	_____
December	10%	_____	_____	_____	_____

a. The previous owners kept excellent records, and the monthly occupancy rates recorded in the table above are time-tested and highly accurate. Use that information to calculate the total revenue Roger can anticipate each month, and enter your results in the table.

b. Assuming that Roger is open for business every month, complete the remainder of the table using the information provided above.

c. According to the **shutdown rule,** Roger's B & B should stay open in a given month only if total revenue from operations that month (exceeds/equals/falls short of) the firm's (total variable cost/total fixed cost/total cost) for the month. Otherwise, the B & B should be shut down.

d. Roger has figured out he really should shut down part of the year. According to the shutdown rule, Roger maximizes his profit if he shuts down the B & B for the months of _____. He should remain open during the months of _____.

e. If Roger follows the guidelines in part (d) and shuts down part of the year, his total profit will be _____. If, instead, he stays open year round his total profit will be only _____.

15-MINUTE PRACTICE TEST

Set a timer, giving yourself just 15 minutes to answer all of the following questions. To see what you *really* know and remember, take the test at least a day *after* you've read the chapter in the text and completed the exercises in this study guide.

Multiple Choice: Circle the letter in front of the single best answer.

1. Economic profit is
    a. the same as accounting profit.
    b. the difference between the firm's total revenue and its explicit costs.
    c. the difference between the firm's marginal revenue and marginal cost.
    d. all of the above.
    e. none of the above.

2. The demand curve facing the firm shows us, for any given output level,
    a. total revenue.
    b. total cost.
    c. the minimum price the firm can charge.
    d. the maximum price the firm can charge.
    e. none of the above.

3. The firm maximizes profit by producing the output level at which
    a. total revenue equals total cost.
    b. total revenue minus total cost is greatest.
    c. marginal revenue minus marginal cost is greatest.
    d. total revenue is as high as possible.
    e. price is as high as possible.

4. According to the marginal approach to profit, a firm should take any action that
   a. increases marginal revenue.
   b. increases total revenue.
   c. decreases total cost.
   d. decreases marginal cost.
   e. adds more to revenue than to cost.

Questions 5–8 refer to the following data, derived from the demand curve facing the firm

P	Q	TC
$100	4	$350
$ 90	5	$375
$ 80	6	$425
$ 70	7	$500

5. For this firm, the marginal revenue when price is lowered from $100 to $90 is
   a. $50.
   b. $90.
   c. $100.
   d. $400.
   e. $450.

6. At which output level or levels could this firm make a positive economic profit?
   a. 4
   b. 5
   c. 6
   d. All of the above.
   e. None of the above.

7. For this firm, as output increases from 4 to 5 to 6 to 7,
   a. marginal cost increases.
   b. marginal cost decreases.
   c. marginal revenue increases.
   d. total revenue decreases.
   e. total revenue remains unchanged.

8. For this firm, the profit maximizing output level is
   a. 4.
   b. 5.
   c. 6.
   d. 7.
   e. none of the above—the firm should shut down.

9. According to the shut-down rule, a firm should shut down in the short run whenever—at the output level where MR = MC—
   a. total cost exceeds total revenue.
   b. total cost exceeds marginal cost.
   c. total fixed cost exceeds total revenue.
   d. total variable cost exceeds total revenue.
   e. total fixed cost exceeds total variable cost.

10. Which of the following typically leads to the principal-agent problem?
    a. The agent is easily monitored by the principal.
    b. The principal is easily monitored by the agent.
    c. The agent cannot be easily monitored by the principal.
    d. The principal cannot be easily monitored by the agent.
    e. Both the principal and the agent can easily monitor each other.

True/False: For each of the following statements, circle T if the statement is true or F if the statement is false.

T   F   1. While economists can explain why there are payments for land, labor and capital, they have not been able to explain why there are profits.

T   F   2. Economic profit can be defined as total revenue minus all explicit and implicit costs to the firm.

T   F   3. A friendly takeover occurs when a firm's own stockholders vote to replace the firm's management.

T   F   4. Whenever marginal revenue is positive, increasing output by one unit will increase total revenue.

T   F   5. The output level that maximizes profit is the same as the output level that maximizes total revenue.

T   F   6. When MR and MC cross at two places, the profit-maximizing output level is the one at which the MC curve crosses the MR curve from above.

T   F   7. A useful rule for deciding whether to increase output is to compare the gain in revenue with the average cost of production.

T   F   8. No matter how large the loss, a firm should always stay open in the short run if its total revenue is sufficient to cover the total variable cost of production.

CHAPTER 8

PERFECT COMPETITION

Fill in each blank with the appropriate word or phrase from the list provided in the word bank. (For a challenge, fill in as many blanks as you can *without* using the word bank.)

_____ 1. The characteristics of a market that influence how trading takes place.

_____ 2. A market structure in which there are many buyers and sellers, the product is standardized, and sellers can easily enter or exit the market.

_____ 3. Any firm that treats the price of its product as given and beyond its control.

_____ 4. The price at which a firm is indifferent between producing and shutting down.

_____ 5. A curve that shows the quantity of output a competitive firm will produce at different prices.

_____ 6. A curve indicating the quantity of output that all sellers in a market will produce at different prices.

_____ 7. Another name for zero economic profit.

_____ 8. A curve indicating the quantity of output that all sellers in a market will produce at different prices, after all long-run adjustments have taken place.

_____ 9. An industry in which the long-run supply curve slopes upward because each firm's ATC curve shifts upward as industry output increases.

_____ 10. An industry in which the long-run supply curve is horizontal because each firm's ATC curve is unaffected by changes in industry output.

_____ 11. An industry in which the long-run supply curve slopes downward because each firm's ATC curve shifts downward as industry output increases.

_____ 12. Price changes that cause firms to change their production to more closely match consumer demand.

Word Bank

constant cost industry

decreasing cost industry

firm's supply curve

increasing cost industry

long-run supply curve

market signals

market structure

market supply curve

normal profit

price taker

perfect competition

shutdown price

CHAPTER HIGHLIGHTS

Fill in each blank with the appropriate word or phrase. If you have difficulty, review the chapter and then try again.

1. By _____ , we mean all the characteristics of a market that influence the behavior of buyers and sellers when they come together to trade.

2. Perfect competition is a market structure with three important characteristics: (1) a large number of buyers and sellers, and each buyrs or sells only a tiny fracdtion of the total quantity in the market; (2) sellers offer a _____ product; and (3) sellers can easily _____ and _____ the market.

3. In a perfectly competitive market, the number of buyers and sellers is so large that no individual decision maker can significantly affect the _____ of the product by changing the quantity it buys or sells.

4. A perfectly competitive firm faces a _____ constraint like any other firm. The cost of producing any given level of output depends on the firm's production _____ and the prices it must pay for its _____ .

5. In perfect competition, the firm is a _____; it treats the _____ of its output as given.

6. For a competitive firm, marginal revenue at each quantity is the same as the _____. For this reason, the _____ curve and the _____ are the same—a horizontal line at the market price.

7. A firm earns a profit whenever price is greater than _____. Its total profit at the best output level equals the area of a rectangle with height equal to the distance between _____ and _____, and width equal to the level of output.

8. A firm suffers a loss whenever _____ is greater than P at the best level of output. Its total loss equals the area of a rectangle with height equal to the distance between _____ and _____, and width equal to the level of output.

9. As the price of output changes, the firm will slide along its _____ curve in deciding how much to produce.

10. The competitive firm's supply curve has two parts. For all prices above the minimum point on its _____ curve, the supply curve coincides with the _____ curve. For all prices below the minimum point on the _____ curve, the firm will shut down, so its supply curve becomes a vertical line at _____ units of output.

11. In the _____ run, the number of firms in the industry is fixed.

12. To obtain the _____, simply add up the quantities of output supplied by all firms in the market at each _____.

13. In a competitive market, economic _____ and _____ are the forces driving long-run change. The expectation of continued _____ causes outsiders to enter the market; the expectation of continued _____ causes firms in the market to exit.

14. In a competitive market, positive economic profit continues to attract new entrants until economic profit is reduced to _____.

15. In a competitive market, economic losses continue to cause exit until the losses are reduced to _____.

16. In the long run, every competitive firm will earn _____ profit, which is another name for zero economic profit.

17. In long-run equilibrium, every competitive firm will select its plant size and output level so that it operates at the minimum point of its _____ curve.

18. At each competitive firm in long-run equilibrium, P = _____ = minimum
    ATC = minimum _____.

19. The _____ curve shows the relationship between market price and market
    quantity produced after all long-run adjustments have taken place.

20. In a market economy, price changes act as _____, ensuring that the
    pattern of production matches the pattern of consumer demands. When demand increases,
    a(n) _____ in price signals firms to _____ the market,
    increasing industry output. When demand decreases, a(n) _____ in price
    signals firms to _____ the market, decreasing industry output.

21. Under pure competition, a technological advance causes the market supply curve to shift to
    the _____ , causing the market price to _____. In the
    short run, early adopters may enjoy economic profit, but in the long run, all adopters will
    earn _____ economic profit. Firms that refuse to use the new technology
    will not survive.

IMPORTANT CONCEPTS

Write a brief answer below each of the following questions.

1. List the three characteristics that define a perfectly competitive market.

   a.

   b.

   c.

2. Which of the three characteristics of perfect competition ensures that economic profit is
   driven to zero in the long run?

3. Indicate whether this statement is true or false, and give a brief explanation: "Under perfect competition, the market demand curve is horizontal."

4. State the shut-down rule for a competitive firm, using the market price of the firm's output as a guide. (Your rule should tell us when the firm should shut down, and when the firm should stay open.)

5. What is the key difference between the "market supply curve" and the "long-run supply curve" for an industry?

6. What are the differences between an increasing cost industry, a decreasing cost industry, and a constant cost industry?

SKILLS AND TOOLS

For each of the following items, follow the instructions, write the correct answer in the blank, or circle the correct answers.

1. Wired is one of many small producers in the perfectly competitive copper wire market. The table below provides data on Wired's output in coils of wire per week, and its total costs in dollars.

Output	TR	TC	MR	MC	Profit
0	_____	6			_____
			_____	_____	
1	_____	7			_____
			_____	_____	
2	_____	10			_____
			_____	_____	
3	_____	15			_____
			_____	_____	
4	_____	22			_____
			_____	_____	
5	_____	31			_____
			_____	_____	
6	_____	42			_____
			_____	_____	
7	_____	55			_____
			_____	_____	
8	_____	70			_____
			_____	_____	
9	_____	87			_____
			_____	_____	
10	_____	106			_____

a. If the market price of wire is currently $12 per coil, compute marginal revenue, marginal cost and total profit at each level of output. Fill in the table.

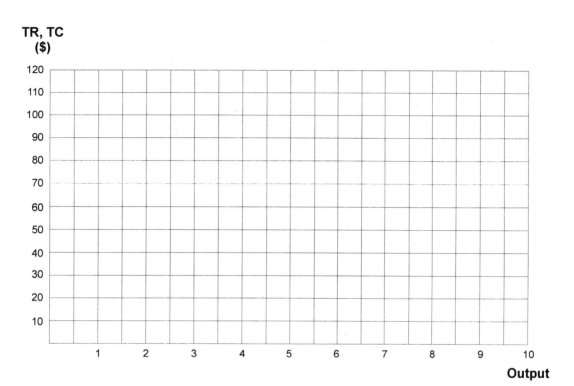

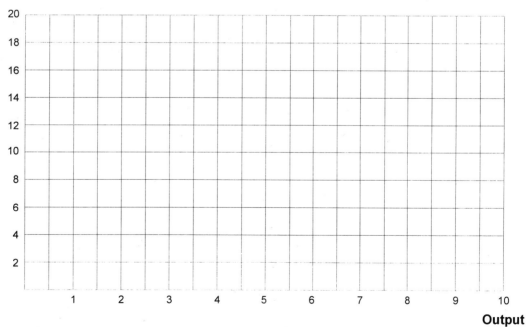

b. In the topmost grid, plot Wired's total revenue and total cost curves. Plot Wired's marginal revenue and marginal cost curves in the bottom grid. (Remember to observe the convention of plotting marginal values at the midpoint of the range over which you calculate them.)

c. To maximize profit, Wired should produce _____ coils per week. When it does, it will realize maximum total profit of _____ dollars per week. In the topmost grid, this amount of profit corresponds to the (horizontal/vertical) distance between the TR and the TC curves at an output of _____ coils per week. In the bottom grid, we can see that when output is less than the profit-maximizing level, marginal cost is (greater than/equal to/less than) marginal revenue. When output is greater than the profit-maximizing level, marginal cost is (greater than/equal to/less than) marginal revenue. When Wired is producing the profit-maximizing output of _____ cases per week, marginal revenue is (greater than/equal to/less than) marginal cost.

2. A firm sells its output in a perfectly competitive market. Its ATC, AVC, and MC curves are drawn below.

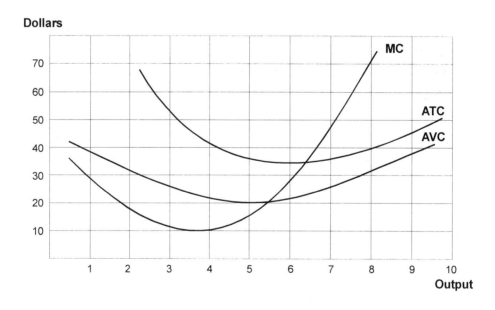

a. When the market price of output is $50 per unit, this firm will maximize its profit by producing approximately _____ units. At that level of output, profit per unit will be approximately (5/15/25) dollars. Total profit will be approximately (35/105/175) dollars.

b. If the market price of output rises to $60, the firm will maximize profit by (decreasing/ increasing) its output to approximately _____ units. Its profit per unit will (rise/fall) to between (30 and 35/20 and 25/10 and 15) dollars, and its total profit will (rise/fall) to between (225 and 263/150 and 188/75 and 113) dollars

c. If the market price should fall to $30, the firm's best course of action in the short run is to (keep producing/shut down because its total revenue (exceeds/equals/falls below) its total variable cost. The firm will maximize profit by producing approximately _____ units of output. At a price of $30, producing this output, the firm will earn (negative/positive/zero) profits in the short run.

d. If the market price should fall to $15, it (is/is not) possible for the firm to earn positive profit. To maximize profit, the firm should (shut down/produce what it can) in the short run.

3. For the firm in the previous question, complete the following short-run supply schedule, indicating the quantity this firm would supply to the market at different market prices. Then plot the firm's short-run supply curve in the grid provided.

Market Price	Quantity Supplied
$70	_____
60	_____
50	_____
40	_____
30	_____
20	_____
10	_____
5	_____

4. Regional monthly market demand for alfalfa sprouts is depicted in the panel on the left
    below. The marginal cost curve for a typical sprout producer is depicted in the panel on the
    right. The minimum level of average variable cost is zero. We know that the regional market
    for alfalfa sprouts is perfectly competitive.

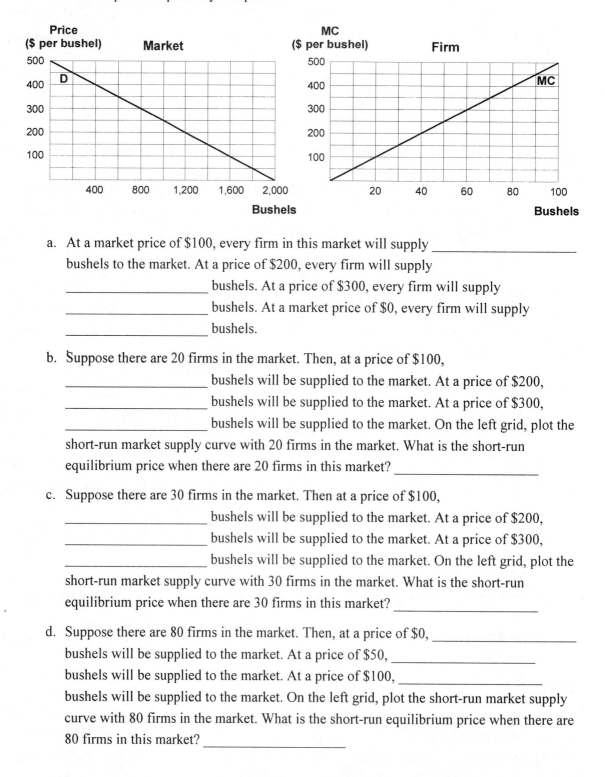

a. At a market price of $100, every firm in this market will supply _____
    bushels to the market. At a price of $200, every firm will supply
    _____ bushels. At a price of $300, every firm will supply
    _____ bushels. At a market price of $0, every firm will supply
    _____ bushels.

b. Suppose there are 20 firms in the market. Then, at a price of $100,
    _____ bushels will be supplied to the market. At a price of $200,
    _____ bushels will be supplied to the market. At a price of $300,
    _____ bushels will be supplied to the market. On the left grid, plot the
    short-run market supply curve with 20 firms in the market. What is the short-run
    equilibrium price when there are 20 firms in this market? _____

c. Suppose there are 30 firms in the market. Then at a price of $100,
    _____ bushels will be supplied to the market. At a price of $200,
    _____ bushels will be supplied to the market. At a price of $300,
    _____ bushels will be supplied to the market. On the left grid, plot the
    short-run market supply curve with 30 firms in the market. What is the short-run
    equilibrium price when there are 30 firms in this market? _____

d. Suppose there are 80 firms in the market. Then, at a price of $0, _____
    bushels will be supplied to the market. At a price of $50, _____
    bushels will be supplied to the market. At a price of $100, _____
    bushels will be supplied to the market. On the left grid, plot the short-run market supply
    curve with 80 firms in the market. What is the short-run equilibrium price when there are
    80 firms in this market? _____

5. Consider the perfectly competitive market and firm depicted below.

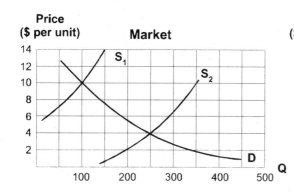 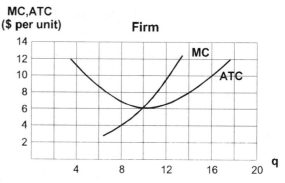

a. When the short-run market supply curve is S_1, the short-run equilibrium price in this market will be _____ dollars. At this price, the market (is/is not) in long-run equilibrium. When market supply is S_1, firms earn (positive profit/negative profit/zero profit). This will cause other firms to (enter this market/exit this market/ neither enter nor exit this market). This will (shift market supply to the right/shift market supply to the left/leave the market supply curve unchanged), causing market price to (fall/rise/remain unchanged) in the long run.

b. When the short-run market supply curve is S_2, the short-run equilibrium price in this market will be _____ dollars. At this price, the market (is/is not) in long-run equilibrium. When market supply is S_2, firms earn (positive profit/negative profit/zero profit). This will cause other firms to (enter this market/exit this market/neither enter nor exit this market). This will (shift market supply to the right/shift market supply to the left/leave the market supply curve unchanged), causing market price to (fall/rise/ remain unchanged) in the long run.

c. In the long run, entry and exit will occur until market supply intersects market demand at a price of _____. When equilibrium price is this level, firms will (earn positive profit/make losses/earn zero economic profit). Firms will then (enter/exit/neither enter nor exit) this market, and the market (will/will not) be in long run equilibrium.

15-MINUTE PRACTICE TEST

Set a timer, giving yourself just 15 minutes to answer all of the following questions. To see what you *really* know and remember, take the test at least a day *after* you've read the chapter in the text and completed the exercises in this study guide.

Multiple Choice: Circle the letter in front of the single best answer.

1. Which of the following is a characteristic of perfect competition?
   a. There are many buyers and sellers.
   b. The firm faces a downward sloping demand curve.
   c. Every seller offers a different product from other sellers.
   d. All of the above.
   e. None of the above.

2. Which of the following is a condition for profit-maximization in a perfectly competitive firm?
   a. $TR = TC$
   b. $P = MC$
   c. $P = AVC$
   d. All of the above.
   c. None of the above.

3. A perfectly competitive firm earns positive economic profit whenever
   a. $P > MC$.
   b. $P > MR$.
   c. $MR > P$.
   d. $P > ATC$.
   e. $ATC > MC$.

4. For a competitive firm, profit per unit of output is equal to
   a. $P - ATC$.
   b. $MC - ATC$.
   c. $TR - TC$.
   d. $P - AVC$.
   e. $MR - MC$.

5. Which of the following statements about perfect competition is *false*?
   a. In the short run, the number of firms in the industry is fixed.
   b. All firms in the industry produce a standardized product.
   c. Each firm determines the price at which it will sell its output.
   d. For a perfectly competitive firm, marginal revenue is the same as market price.
   e. There are no significant barriers to entry or exit.

6. In a perfectly competitive market, an increase in demand will, in the long run, generally cause:
   a. an increase in price.
   b. an increase in market output.
   c. an increase in the number of firms.
   d. all of the above.
   e. none of the above.

7. A perfectly competitive firm should shut down in the short run whenever, at the best possible output,
   a. $P < ATC$
   b. $P < AVC$
   c. $P < MR$
   d. $P < ATC + AVC$
   e. none of the above

8. A technological advance in a perfectly competitive market will, in the long run, lead to
   a. greater profit at each firm.
   b. higher prices charged by each firm.
   c. a leftward shift of the market supply curve.
   d. all of the above.
   e. none of the above.

9. In a perfectly competitive market, an increase in the price of a variable input will cause an upward shift in each firm's
   a. MC curve.
   b. ATC curve.
   c. AVC curve.
   d. All of the above.
   e. None of the above.

10. In a competitive industry, a rightward shift of the demand curve will cause
    a. economic profit for each firm in the long run.
    b. economic loss for each firm in the long run.
    c. economic profit for each firm in the short run, and entry in the long run.
    d. economic profit for each firm in the short run, and exit in the long run.
    e. economic loss for each firm in the short run, and exit in the long run.

True/False: For each of the following statements, circle T if the statement is true or F if the statement is false.

T   F   1. Since the assumptions of perfect competition are rarely completely satisfied in practice, the perfectly competitive model is rarely used by economists.

T   F   2. Under perfect competition, the firm's supply curve is horizontal.

T   F   3. Under perfect competition, in long run equilibrium, accounting profit may be greater than zero.

T   F   4. Under perfect competition, an increase in the market price will increase each firm's marginal revenue.

T   F   5. In a perfectly competitive, increasing cost industry, a *leftward* shift of the demand curve will—in the long run—cause the market price to rise.

T   F   6. Under perfect competition, in long-run equilibrium, P = MC = AVC.

T   F   7. Under perfect competition, a technological advance enabling firms to produce the same output at lower cost will cause the market supply curve to shift rightward.

T   F   8. A perfectly competitive firm should shut down whenever the market price is lower than the minimum point on the AVC curve.

CHAPTER 9

MONOPOLY

Fill in each blank with the appropriate word or phrase from the list provided in the word bank. (For a challenge, fill in as many blanks as you can *without* using the word bank.)

_____ 1. The only seller of a good or service that has no close substitutes.

_____ 2. The market in which a monopoly firm operates.

_____ 3. A market in which, due to economies of scale, one firm can operate at lower average cost than can two or more firms.

_____ 4. A temporary grant of monopoly rights over a new product or scientific discovery.

_____ 5. A grant of exclusive rights to sell a literary, musical, or artistic work.

_____ 6. A government-granted right to be the sole seller of a product or service.

_____ 7. Any costly action a firm undertakes to establish or maintain its monopoly status.

_____ 8. A monopoly firm that is limited to charging the same price for each unit of output sold.

_____ 9. Charging different prices to different customers for reasons other than differences in production costs.

_____ 10. Charging each customer the most he or she would be willing to pay for each unit purchased.

Word Bank

copyright   patent
government franchise   prefect price discrimination
monopoly firm   price discrimination
monopoly market   rent-seeking activity
natural monopoly   single-price monopoly

CHAPTER HIGHLIGHTS

Fill in each blank with the appropriate word or phrase. If you have difficulty, review the chapter and then try again.

1. A monopoly firm is the only seller of a good or service with no _____.

2. A natural monopoly exists when, due to _____, one firm can produce at lower _____ than can two or more firms.

3. In dealing with intellectual property, the government strikes a compromise: it allows the creators of intellectual property to enjoy a (an) _____ and earn _____ , but only for a limited period of time. Once the time is up, other sellers are allowed to enter the market, and it is hoped that competition among them will _____ prices.

4. A monopolist, like any firm, strives to _____.

5. A monopoly, like any firm, also faces constraints. For any level of output it might produce, total cost is determined by (1) it's _____ and (2) the price it must pay for its _____. And forany level of output it might produce, the maximum price it can charge is determined by the market _____ curve for its product.

6. When any firm—including a monopoly—faces a downward sloping demand curve for its product, _____ will be less than the price of output, so the _____ curve will lie below the demand curve.

7. A monopoly will never produce a level of output at which its marginal revenue is _____.

8. To maximize profit, a (single price) monopoly should produce the level of output where _____ = MR, and the _____ curve crosses the MR curve from _____.

9. A (single price) monopoly earns a profit whenever P > _____, and suffers a loss whenever P < _____.

10. Any firm—including a (single-price) monopoly—should shut down if P < _____ at the output level where MR = _____.

11. *Unlike* perfectly competitive firms, monopolies may earn economic profit in the _____ run.

12. We do not expect to find privately owned monopolies whose long run economic profit is _____.

13. All else being equal, we can expect a monopoly market to have a higher _____ and a lower _____ than a perfectly competitive market.

14. The monopolization of a competitive industry has two opposing effects. First, for any given technology of production, monopolization leads to _____ prices and _____ output. Second, changes in the technology of production made possible under monopoly may lead to _____ prices and _____ output. The ultimate effect on prices and output can go either way.

15. Any costly action a firm undertakes to establish or maintain its monopoly status is called _____, and tends to reduce the monopoly's _____.

16. A monopolist will react to an increase in demand by _____ output, _____ price, and earning a _____ profit.

17. Price discrimination occurs when a firm charges different prices to different customers for reasons other than differences in _____.

18. Under _____ price discrimination, the firm charges each customer the most he or she would be willing to pay for each unit he or she buys.

19. For a _____ price discriminator, marginal revenue is equal to the price of the additional unit sold. Thus, the firm's MR curve is the same as its _____ curve.

IMPORTANT CONCEPTS

Write a brief answer below each of the following questions.

1. List four distinct types of barriers to entry that can explain the existence of a monopoly. (Hint: two of these barriers are created by government).

    a.

    b.

    c.

    d.

2. Under perfect competition, economic profit may exist in the short run, but not the long run. Do the same results hold for a monopoly? Explain briefly.

3. List two reasons why many monopolies—in spite of barriers to entry—earn zero economic profit over the long run.

    a.

    b.

4. Indicate whether this statement is true or false, and explain briefly: "Since there are no close substitutes for its product, a privately-owned monopoly firm will maximize profit by charging as high a price as the government or public sentiment will allow."

5. List the three conditions that must be satisfied for successful price discrimination.

   a.

   b.

   c.

6. Indicate whether this statement is true or false, and explain briefly: "The supply curve for a single-price monopoly firm is upward sloping."

SKILLS AND TOOLS

1. Margaret managed to maneuver a monopoly in the market for mailbox magnets in metropolitan Muskegon. Monthly market demand is graphed below.

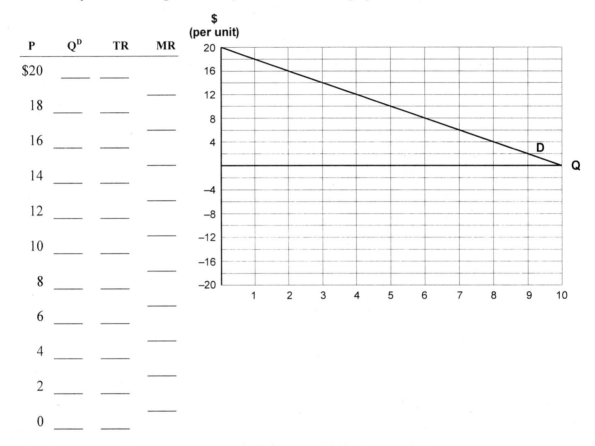

P	Q^D	TR	MR
$20	___	___	
			___
18	___	___	
			___
16	___	___	
			___
14	___	___	
			___
12	___	___	
			___
10	___	___	
			___
8	___	___	
			___
6	___	___	
			___
4	___	___	
			___
2	___	___	
			___
0	___	___	

a. Read Margaret's demand curve, and complete the first column in the table. Then complete the rest of the table.

b. Plot Margaret's marginal revenue curve. (Remember to plot the marginal value at the midpoint of the range over which you've calculated it.)

c. When Margaret is selling two mailbox magnets per month, marginal revenue is (positive/ negative/zero). This tells us that her revenue will (increase/decrease remain unchanged) if she sells an additional magnet.

d. When Margaret is selling seven mailbox magnets per month, marginal revenue is (positive/negative/zero). This tells us that her revenue will (increase/decrease/remain unchanged) if she sells an additional magnet.

e. Margaret is a profit maximizer, and she will always pick a level of output that maximizes her profit. Even though we know nothing about Margaret's costs, we know she will never produce an output where marginal revenue is (positive/negative/zero). Thus, no matter what her costs are, we can be sure Margaret will never produce more that _____ magnets per month.

2. Margaret's mother, Molly, sells antique movie magazines. Molly knows her marginal cost curve and it is plotted below. She does not know what her demand curve looks like, although she has collected the bits of evidence on price, quantity demanded, and total revenue per month reported in the table below.

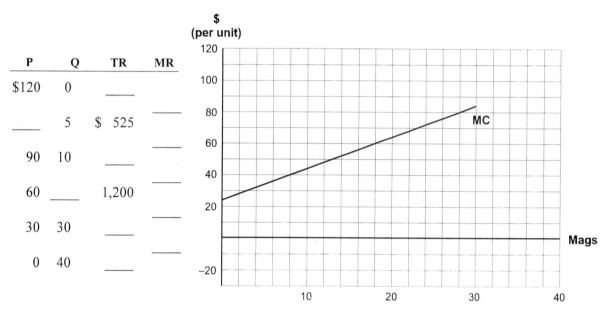

P	Q	TR	MR
$120	0	____	
			____
____	5	$ 525	
			____
90	10	____	
			____
60	____	1,200	
			____
30	30	____	
			____
0	40	____	

a. Complete the table.

b. Plot Molly's demand curve and marginal revenue curve. (Remember to plot the marginal values at the midpoint of the range over which you calculate them).

c. To maximize her profit, how many movie mags should Molly sell each month? _____ At that level of output, marginal revenue will equal approximately _____ dollars, and marginal cost will equal approximately _____ dollars. Molly should sell these magazines at a price of approximately _____ dollars.

d. If Molly were to sell one more movie mag beyond the profit maximizing output you found, marginal revenue would (be greater than/less than/equal to) marginal cost, and her profit would (rise/fall/remain unchanged).

3. A monopolist has the cost, demand and marginal revenue curve depicted below.

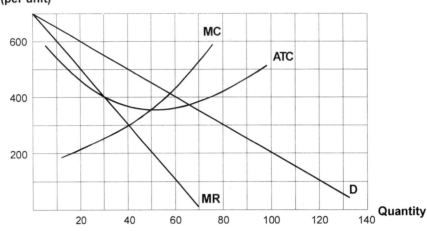

a. What output maximizes the monopolist's profit? _____

b. What is marginal revenue at the profit-maximizing output? _____ What is
    marginal cost at the profit maximizing output? _____ At the profit
    maximizing output, marginal revenue (is greater than/equal to/less than) marginal cost.

c. What price does the monopolist charge? _____

d. What is average total cost at the monopoly equilibrium? _____

e. What is profit per unit in the monopoly equilibrium? _____

f. What is the monopolist's total profit in equilibrium? _____

4. Monty just invented a new board game—he calls it "Slopes and 'Cepts." Market research
   indicates that demand for this game is given by

$$P = 56 - .25Q,$$

and Monty's marginal revenue is given by the equation:

$$MR = 56 - 0.5Q$$

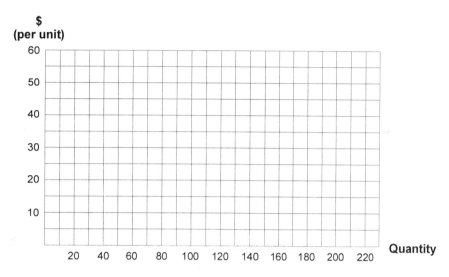

a. Plot Monty's demand curve and marginal revenue curves on the grid above. Label each one clearly.

b. Right now, the marginal cost of producing each game is constant and equal to $30 no matter how many games Monty produces. Plot the corresponding marginal cost curve on the grid.

c. How many games should Monty produce to maximize his profit? _____
How much should he charge for each game? _____

d. One day, the price of the cardboard used in producing board games rises. Monty now finds that the marginal cost of producing a game has increased to $40. Plot Monty's new marginal cost curve on the grid above. How many games should Monty produce now? _____ How much should he charge? _____

e. Looking back over (c) and (d), we can see that when marginal cost rose by $10, the price Monty charges rose by only _____ dollars. In this situation, Monty's best course of action was (to/ to not) pass along to his customers the entire increase in his costs.

5. You may have noticed a curious fact while you were working on the last problem: Monty's demand curve and marginal revenue curve share the same vertical intercept, and the marginal revenue curve is exactly twice as steep as the demand curve.

This is no coincidence. In fact, it is the result of a general rule that governs the relationship between the marginal revenue and demand curves when the demand curve is a straight line. Specifically, it can be shown that when a firm's demand curve is linear and can be written in the form:

$$\text{Demand:} \quad P = a - bQ$$

the firm's associated marginal revenue curve will have the form:

$$\text{Marginal revenue:} \quad MR = a - 2bQ.$$

a. If we were to graph the equation for demand displayed above, the demand curve would intercept the vertical (dollars) axis at _____ . The slope of the demand curve would be _____ . The demand curve would cross the horizontal quantity axis at a quantity of _____. (Hint: What is the value of P when the demand curve hits the horizontal axis?)

b. If we were to graph the marginal revenue equation displayed above, the marginal revenue curve would intercept the vertical (dollars) axis at _____ . The slope of the marginal revenue curve would be _____ . The marginal revenue curve would intercept the horizontal (quantity) axis at a quantity of _____.

c. Making use of the rule we just described, fill in the blanks

Demand	Marginal Revenue
$P = 34 - 4Q$	$MR = \underline{\quad} - 8Q$
$P = \underline{\quad} - 15Q$	$MR = 28 - 30Q$
$P = 72 - 12Q$	$MR = 72 - \underline{\quad}Q$
$P = 12 - 8Q$	$MR = \underline{\quad} - \underline{\quad}Q$
$P = \underline{\quad} - \underline{\quad}Q$	$MR = 105 - 50Q$

6. When old Doc rode into town on the stage last month, he was the first and only surgeon to set foot in this part of the country. It didn't take him long to learn that if he charged $1,000 for a hernia operation, no one would have the procedure. If, however, he cut the price to $750, the banker would have his done right away. If he charged only $500, both the banker and the grocer would have the procedure, while if he went as low as $250, the ranch hand would get one, too. Of course, if he repaired hernias for free, even the schoolteacher would get one done, but let's be realistic—Doc can't just give these things away. In fact, he figures that the average total cost he incurs for each hernia he repairs is constant and equal to $125.

P	Q^D
$1,000	_____
750	_____
500	_____
250	_____
0	_____

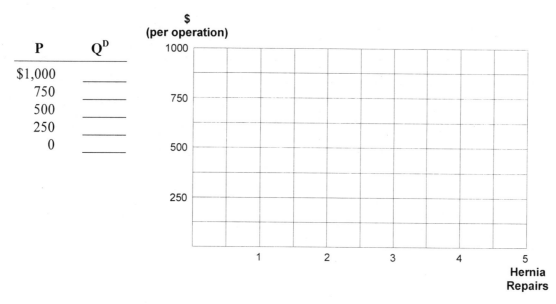

a. If Doc were to charge everyone the same price for an operation, complete the table telling how many operations would be demanded at each listed price. Using the information in this table, plot the demand curve Doc faces.

b. Plot Doc's average total cost (ATC) curve.

c. If Doc decides to charge everyone the same price of $250 for a hernia repair:

How many repairs will he perform? _____

How much revenue will he earn? _____

What will be Doc's total cost? _____

How much profit will he earn? _____

One day, when the fog cleared, Doc had a realization: Since he knows who will pay what, he thought he might be able to make *more* money by price discriminating among his buyers.

d. If, for otherwise indistinguishable hernia repairs, Doc charges the banker $750, the grocer $500, and the ranch hand $250:

How many repairs will he perform? _____.

How much revenue will he earn? _____

What will be Doc's total cost? _____

How much profit will he earn? _____

e. Does Doc make more profit when he price discriminates or when he charges everyone the same price? _____

15-MINUTE PRACTICE TEST

Set a timer, giving yourself just 15 minutes to answer all of the following questions. To see what you *really* know and remember, take the test at least a day *after* you've read the chapter in the text and completed the exercises in this study guide.

Multiple Choice: Circle the letter in front of the single, best answer.

1. A monopoly firm is the only seller of a good or service with
    a. no barriers to entry.
    b. no close substitutes.
    c. no close complements.
    d. no government involvement.
    e. none of the above.

2. Which of the following can explain why a market becomes a monopoly rather than a purely competitive market?
    a. Economies of scale
    b. Easy entry and exit
    c. Standardized product
    d. Downward sloping market demand curve
    e. Horizontal demand curve

3. For a single-price monopoly, the marginal revenue curve
    a. is horizontal.
    b. is vertical.
    c. lies below the demand curve.
    d. lies above the demand curve.
    e. is the same as the demand curve.

4. A single-price monopoly will never produce a level of output where

    a. profit is negative.
    b. marginal revenue is negative.
    c. marginal cost is positive.
    d. marginal cost exceeds average total cost.
    e. average total cost exceeds marginal cost.

5. A single-price monopoly should shut down when, at the output level where MR = MC,

    a. MC > ATC.
    b. ATC > MC.
    c. P < ATC.
    d. P < AVC.
    e. ATC < AVC.

6. When a competitive market is monopolized, the result is always

    a. higher prices.
    b. a lower level of output.
    c. the end of rent-seeking activity.
    d. all of the above.
    e. none of the above.

7. When demand for a monopoly's output increases, the monopolist will

    a. raise its price.
    b. increase its output.
    c. earn greater profit.
    d. All of the above.
    e. None of the above.

8. Which of the following is a requirement for successful price discrimination?

    a. Inelastic demand for the firm's output
    b. The ability to know exactly how much each consumer is willing to pay
    c. The ability to prevent low-price customers from reselling to high-price customers
    d. All of the above
    e. None of the above

9. When the conditions for price discrimination are satisfied, price discrimination

    a. always harms consumers and benefits the firm.
    b. always benefits the firm, and may help or harm consumers.
    c. always benefits both consumers and the firm.
    d. always harms both consumers and the firm.
    e. always harms the firm, and may help or harm consumers.

10. For a perfect price discriminator, the MR curve
    a. is vertical.
    b. is horizontal.
    c. lies above the demand curve.
    d. lies below the demand curve.
    e. is the same as the demand curve.

True/False: For each of the following statements, circle T if the statement is true or F if the statement is false.

T   F   1. In dealing with intellectual property, government grants patents and copyrights, knowing that this will permanently raise the price above the competitive price and create an unending stream of profits for the creator.

T   F   2. Just like purely competitive firms, monopoly firms can earn economic profit in the long run.

T   F   3. For a single-price monopoly, the marginal revenue of producing another unit of output is equal to the price at which that unit of output will be sold.

T   F   4. To maximize profit, a single-price monopoly should produce the output level at which P = MC.

T   F   5. A monopoly firm's supply curve is upward sloping.

T   F   6. A (single price) monopoly firm should shut down in the short run whenever P < ATC at the best level of output.

T   F   7. Lobbying government officials to preserve barriers to entry is an example of rent-seeking activity.

T   F   8. Price discrimination always benefits the firm and harms consumers.

CHAPTER 10

MONOPOLISTIC COMPETITION AND OLIGOPOLY

SPEAKING ECONOMICS

Fill in each blank with the appropriate word or phrase from the list provided in the word bank. (For a challenge, fill in as many blanks as you can *without* using the word bank.)

_____ 1. A market structure in which there are many firms selling products that are differentiated, yet are still close substitutes, and in which there is free entry and exit.

_____ 2. Any action a firm takes to increase the demand for its product, other than cutting its price.

_____ 3. A market structure in which a small number of firms are strategically interdependent.

_____ 4. The level of output at which economies of scale are exhausted and minimum LRATC is achieved.

_____ 5. An approach to modeling the strategic interaction of oligopolists in terms of moves and countermoves.

_____ 6. A table showing the payoffs to each of two firms for each pair of strategies they choose.

_____ 7. A strategy that is best for a firm no matter what strategy its competitor chooses.

_____ 8. An oligopoly market with only two sellers.

_____ 9. A situation in which strategically interdependent sellers compete over many time periods.

_____ 10. Cooperation involving direct communication between competing firms about setting price.

_____ 11. A group of firms that select a common price that maximizes total industry profits.

_____ 12. Any form of oligopolistic cooperation that does not involve an explicit agreement.

_____ 13. A game-theoretic strategy of doing to another player this period what he has done to you in the previous period.

_____ 14. A form of tacit collusion in which one firm sets a price that other firms copy.

Word Bank

cartel

dominant strategy

duopoly

explicit collusion

game theory

minimum efficient scale (MES)

monopolistic competition

nonprice competition

oligopoly

payoff matrix

price leadership

repeated play

tacit collusion

tit for tat

CHAPTER HIGHLIGHTS

Fill in the blanks with the appropriate words or phrases. If you have difficulty, review the chapter and then try again.

1. Imperfect competition refers to market structures *between* _____ and _____. In imperfectly competitive markets, there is more than one seller, but still too few to create a _____ market. In addition, imperfectly competitive markets often violate other conditions of _____, such as the requirement of a standardized product or free entry and exit.

2. A monopolistically competitive market has three fundamental characteristics: (1) many small _____ and _____; (2) no significant barriers to _____ or _____; and (3) _____ products.

3. Because it produces a _____ product, a monopolistic competitor faces a _____-sloping demand curve: when it raises its price a modest amount, quantity demanded will _____.

4. Under monopolistic competition, firms can earn positive or negative economic profit in the _____ run. But in the _____ run, free entry and exit will ensure that each firm earns _____ economic profit, just as under perfect competition.

5. In the long run, a monopolistic competitor will operate with _____ capacity—that is, it will produce too little output to achieve _____ cost per unit.

6. Any action a firm takes to increase the demand for its output—other than _____—is called _____ competition.

7. An oligopoly is a market dominated by a small number of strategically _____ firms.

8. A _____ strategy is a strategy that is best for a player regardless of the strategy of the other player.

9. Under monopolistic competition, advertising increases the size of the market. (More units are sold.) But in the long run, each firm earns _____, just as it would if no firm were advertising. The price to the consumer, however, may either rise or fall.

IMPORTANT CONCEPTS

Write a brief answer below each of the following questions.

1. List one characteristic of monopolistic competition which is completely different from perfect competition, and one characteristic which monopolistic competition completely shares with perfect competition.

   a. (Different characteristics) _____

   b. (Shared characteristic) _____

2. Indicate whether this statement is true or false, and explain briefly: "Because monopolistically competitive markets, like perfectly competitive markets, have many firms, each firm faces a horizontal demand curve."

3. What single characteristic differentiates oligopoly from monopolistic competition?

4. List four distinct categories of barriers to entry that can explain the origin of an oligopoly?

   a.

   b.

   c.

   d.

5. What do explicit collusion and tacit collusion have in common? What is the key difference between them?

6. Identify the type of market structure in which each of the following firms sells its output:

   a. One of three clothing stores in a small town. _____

   b. A drug company that holds a patent on the only medicine to treat a particular disease.

      _____

   c. A used car dealer in a large city with several dozen used car dealers.

      _____

   d. A small banana farm in Colombia. _____

7. Indicate whether this statement is true or false, and explain briefly: "Because advertising adds to firms' costs, it always increases the price paid by the consumer."

8. Without using the table in the text, fill in the following summary table for the four market structures:

Characteristic	Perfect Competition	Monopolistic Competition	Oligopoly	Monopoly
Number of Firms (one, few, many, or very many)				
Type of Output (identical or differentiated)				
View of Pricing (price taker or price setter)				
Barriers to Entry or Exit?				
Strategic Interdependence?				
How profit-maximizing output level is found				
Possible values for short-run profit				
Possible values for long-run profit				
Is Advertising Expected?				

SKILLS AND TOOLS

For each of the following items, follow the instructions, write the correct answer in the blank or circle the answer.

1. Roma Deli is typical of many small delicatessen-groceries throughout the country. Its biggest business is the lunch trade, and its biggest selling lunchtime item is the "Heart Stopper," a large sandwich stuffed with prosciutto, ham, salami, provolone, etc. There are many other delis in town, and each has its own specialty similar (but not identical) to the Heart Stopper. Roma Deli's daily cost and demand curves, depicted below, are typical of other local firms. The horizontal axis (Q) measures the number of Heart Stoppers sold daily.

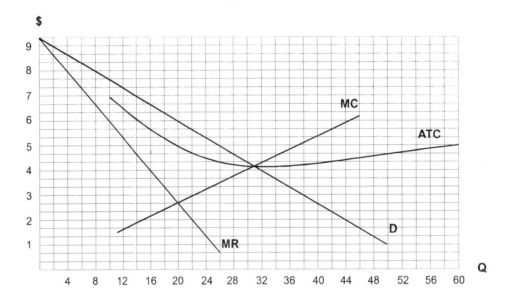

a. In the short run, Roma Deli (can/cannot) make a profit on Heart Stoppers. To (maximize profit/minimize loss), the deli should produce (no output/where marginal revenue exceeds marginal cost/where marginal revenue is equal to marginal cost/where average total cost is equal to marginal cost).

b. In the short run:
    How many Heart Stoppers should Roma Deli sell? _____
    What price should it charge? _____
    What is the average total cost of a Heart Stopper at the profit maximizing output?

    _____
    How much profit will Roma Deli earn each day? _____

c. In the long run, we would expect to see other delis (enter/exit) this market. As those firms (enter/exit), the demand curve facing Roma Deli will (shift leftward/shift rightward/be unaffected). After all adjustments, the deli market will be in long run equilibrium when Roma Deli, and others like it, earn (positive/negative/zero) economic profit.

2. The market demand for crispy rye crackers, recently re-discovered as a healthy snack food, has been estimated to be

$$Q^D = 16,000 - 1,000P,$$

where P is price per case in dollars, and Q is quantity demanded in the market each week.

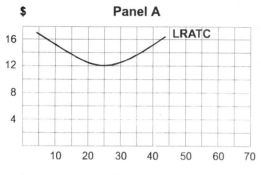

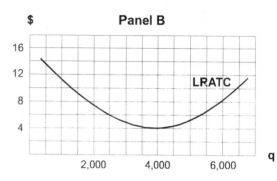

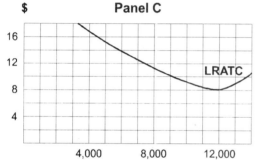

a. Suppose the weekly long-run average total cost curve for a cracker-producing firm is depicted in Panel A. Then the MES of a typical cracker firm will be _____ cases per week. With these costs, the minimum long run average cost of producing a case of crackers is _____. If market price were equal to minimum long run average cost, weekly market demand for crackers would be _____ cases. How many firms, each producing at its minimum efficient scale, would be needed to satisfy market demand at this price? _____ With costs and market demand like this, the market structure we would see in the cracker market most closely resembles (perfect competition/oligopoly/natural monopoly).

b. Suppose the weekly long-run average total cost curve for a cracker-producing firm is depicted in Panel B. Then the MES of a typical cracker firm will be _____ cases per week. With these costs, the minimum long run average cost of producing a case of crackers is _____. If market price were equal to minimum long run average cost, weekly market demand for crackers would be _____ cases. How many firms, each producing at its minimum efficient scale, would be needed to satisfy market demand at this price? _____ With costs and market demand like this, the market structure we would see in the cracker market most closely resembles (perfect competition/oligopoly/natural monopoly).

c. Suppose the weekly long-run average total cost curve for a cracker-producing firm is depicted in Panel C. Then the MES of a typical cracker firm will be _____ cases per week. With these costs, the minimum long run average cost of producing a case of crackers is _____. If market price were equal to minimum long run average cost, weekly market demand for crackers would be _____ cases. How many firms, each producing at its minimum efficient scale, would be needed to satisfy market demand at this price? _____ With costs and market demand like this, the market structure we would see in the cracker market most closely resembles (perfect competition/oligopoly/natural monopoly).

3. Market research shows that consumers like blue—it is a soothing color that most people find attractive. However, red gets attention on the shelf—but too much red can be jarring and turn consumers off. You and your rival must each decide upon the color for your packaging. Both of you have looked at the same research, and both are pretty much in agreement about the following facts.

- If you both use blue, you'll have profit (in thousands) of $100 this year, and your rival will earn $90.
- If you use blue, while she uses red, you'll make $50 but she'll earn $110.
- If you use red and she uses blue, you'll make $120 and she'll only make $40.
- If you both use red, you'll earn $80 and she'll earn $70.

In the following payoff matrix, each row represents one of your strategies, each column one of your rival's strategies.

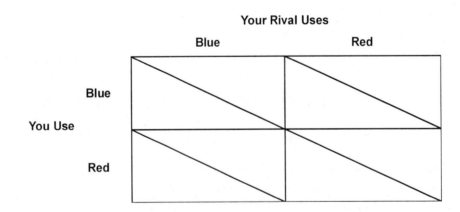

Your Rival Uses

a. Complete the payoff matrix using the information on profits for you and your rival. Put your payoff in the lower left of the cell, and your rival's payoff in the upper right.

b. Which of your strategies is best for you when your rival uses blue? _____ Which is best for you when your rival uses red? _____ Do you have a dominant strategy? _____

c. Now look at the game from your rival's perspective. Which of her strategies is best for her when you use blue? _____ Which is best for her when you use red? _____ Does your rival have a dominant strategy? _____

d. If you and your rival must act independently of one another—each picking your own strategy without knowing the other's choice—what strategy will you choose? _____ What strategy will your rival choose? _____

e. If you and your rival could agree to cooperate, is there a pair of strategies the two of you could agree to follow that would be better for *both of you* than the equilibrium you described in (d)? (Yes/No). To pull it off, you would have to agree to (use blue/use red) and your rival would have to agree to (use blue/use red).

f. If you can count on your rival to keep her word and pursue the strategy agreed upon for her in (e), how much profit do you make if you keep your word, too, and pursue what you agreed to in (e)? _____ How much profit do you make if you cheat, and choose your other strategy despite having agreed not to do so? _____ When do you make the most: when you play by the rules, or when you cheat? _____

g. If your rival can count on you to keep your word and pursue the strategy agreed upon for you in (e), how much profit does she make if she keeps her word, too, and pursues what you agreed to in (e)? _____ How much profit does she make if she cheats, and chooses her other strategy despite having agreed not to do so? _____ When does she make the most: when she plays by the rules, or when she cheats?

_____

4. Folks in Goodgrass, ND, remember when just about anyone could get 40 acres and a mule for practically nothing. In those days, anyone could plant in the spring and get a good crop to market by fall. One year, there were 100 farms, all producing the same grade of wheat. Market demand for that wheat is graphed in the panel on the left below, and the average total cost and marginal cost of a typical farm are drawn in the panel on the right.

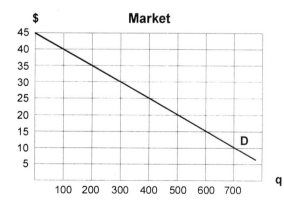

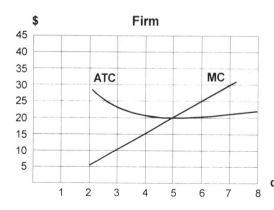

a. If the regional wheat market is perfectly competitive, what will be the long run equilibrium price of wheat? _____ How many bushels will each farm produce at that price? _____ How much economic profit will the typical farm earn? _____

One day down at the Grange Hall, they started talking about forming a regional wheat cartel. All the farmers in Goodgrass would get together and agree to cut back their production in order to raise the price of wheat for everybody. Some folks said that, if everyone pulled together, the price could go as high as $25 a bushel.

b. To get the market price to $25, total market output would have to be _____ bushels. If every one of the 100 farms in Goodgrass produced an equal share of this output, how many bushels would each farm have to produce? _____

c. Obviously, every farm would be better off with the cartel in operation. It may be hard to see in these graphs exactly how much each farm would earn, but because market price of $25 is (greater than/less than/equal to) the farm's average total cost when it produces its output in (b), we know that profit per unit, as well as total profit, will be (positive/negative/zero) for every firm in the cartel.

d. But then Arne Killjoy just had to speak up. He pointed out that if a farm cuts output back to its share of the cartel output, its marginal cost will be _____. If the market price of wheat is $25, it is easy to see that market price will (exceed/equal/be less than) marginal cost at every farm. But then every farmer will think to himself, "If I can just increase my own output a little and sell it all at $25 per bushel, I can make even *more* profit than I'm making in the cartel. And, after all, I'm in the farming business to make money, and the other 99 will probably never notice I'm cheating, so why shouldn't I just go ahead and do it?"

e. Everyone agreed that made sense. But all of them could see that if everyone cheated on the cartel, then everyone would be competing with one another once again and, in the long run, they'd no doubt see the equilibrium market price fall back down to _____ dollars. Then they'd all be back to producing _____ bushels and earning (negative/zero/positive) economic profit once again.

One thing seemed clear to everybody: With the actions of so many farms to coordinate and monitor, collusion was likely to be impossible. That was when they all gave up on the idea and started for the door. . . .

15-MINUTE PRACTICE TEST

Set a timer, giving yourself just 15 minutes to answer all of the following questions. To see what you *really* know and remember, take the test at least a day *after* you've read the chapter in the text and completed the exercises in this study guide.

Multiple Choice: Circle the letter in front of the single best answer.

1. The restaurant industry in a large city most closely resembles the market structure of
   a. perfect competition.
   b. monopolistic competition.
   c. monopoly.
   d. oligopoly with cooperative behavior.
   e. oligopoly without cooperative behavior.

2. Both monopoly and monopolistic competition share which of the following features?
   a. No significant barriers to entry or exit
   b. Zero economic profit in the long run
   c. Downward sloping demand curve
   d. All of the above
   e. None of the above

3. Which of the following is *not* true for monopolistically competitive firms in the *long run*?
   a. Economic profit equals zero.
   b. Price equals average total cost.
   c. Marginal revenue equals marginal cost.
   d. Average total cost is minimized.
   e. Price exceeds marginal revenue.

4. Which of the following is *always* true for monopolistically competitive firms in the *short run*?
   a. Economic profit equals zero.
   b. Price equals average total cost.
   c. Marginal revenue equals marginal cost.
   d. Average total cost is minimized.
   e. Marginal revenue equals price.

5. Under monopolistic competition, firms operate with "excess capacity" in the long run. This means that each firm produces a level of output at which
   a. marginal revenue equals marginal cost.
   b. marginal revenue is greater than marginal cost.
   c. average total cost is greater than its minimum possible value.
   d. price is greater than marginal revenue.
   e. marginal cost is greater than average cost.

6. Which of the following is an example of nonprice competition?

   a. Economic profit attracts entry by new firms.
   b. Economic loss causes exit of existing firms.
   c. A firm produces additional units for which marginal revenue exceeds marginal cost.
   d. A firm cuts back production in order to increase profit.
   e. A firm advertises to gain new customers.

7. A key feature of oligopoly is

   a. differentiated output.
   b. standardized output.
   c. no significant barriers to entry.
   d. strategic interaction.
   e. none of the above.

8. A natural oligopoly is an oligopoly that can be explained by

   a. economies of scale.
   b. zoning regulations.
   c. lobbying of government agencies.
   d. the reputation of existing firms.
   e. none of the above.

9. A dominant strategy in an oligopoly game is a strategy that is best for a player

   a. as long as its competitor follows the same strategy.
   b. as long as its competitor follows a different strategy.
   c. as long as no additional players are allowed to play.
   d. when both players cooperate.
   e. regardless of the strategy of the other player.

10. Price leadership is generally considered an example of

    a. explicit collusion.
    b. tacit collusion.
    c. a tit for tat strategy.
    d. uncooperative behavior.
    e. none of the above.

True/False: For each of the following statements, circle T if the statement is true or F if the statement is false.

T   F   1. Monopolistic competition has three characteristics: a differentiated product, no significant barriers to entry, and few buyers and sellers.

T   F   2. Monopolistic competitors may earn positive economic profit in the short run, but earn zero economic profit in the long run.

T   F   3. Under both perfect competition and monopolistic competition, price equals minimum average total cost in the long run.

T　F　4. A market in which there are 100 firms, each with a 1 percent share of the total market, would most likely be considered an oligopoly.

T　F　5. A natural oligopoly occurs when a firm achieves its minimum efficient scale (MES) at an output level that can supply the entire market.

T　F　6. Cheating on a collusive agreement is more likely when firms can easily observe other firms' prices.

T　F　7. Advertising about superior service is an example of nonprice competition.

T　F　8. Game theory analysis suggests that airlines choose *not* to advertise their safety records because they are cooperating.

CHAPTER 11

THE LABOR MARKET

Fill in the blank with the appropriate word or phrase from the list provided in the word bank. (For a challenge, fill in as many blanks as you can *without* using the word bank.)

_____ 1. Markets in which firms sell goods and services to households or other firms.

_____ 2. Markets in which households sell land, labor and natural resources to firms.

_____ 3. A market with many indistinguishable sellers of labor and many buyers, with no barriers to entry or exit.

_____ 4. The demand for an input that arises from, and varies with, the demand for the product it helps to produce.

_____ 5. Any firm that takes the market wage as a given when making employment decisions.

_____ 6. The change in revenue from hiring one more worker.

_____ 7. A curve indicating the total number of workers all firms in a labor market want to employ at each wage rate.

_____ 8. An input whose utilization increases the marginal product of another input.

_____ 9. An input whose utilization decreases the marginal product of another input.

_____ 10. The lowest wage rate at which an individual would supply labor to a particular labor market.

_____ 11. A curve indicating the number of people who want jobs in a labor market at each wage rate.

_____ 12. A curve indicating how many people will want to work in a labor market at each wage rate, after full adjustment to a wage change.

_____ 13. The quantity of labor demanded exceeds the quantity
supplied at the prevailing wage rate.

_____ 14. The quantity of labor supplied exceeds the quantity
demanded at the prevailing wage rate.

Word Bank

complementary input   market labor demand curve
derived demand   perfectly competitive labor market
labor shortage   product markets
labor supply curve   reservation wage
labor surplus   factor markets
long-run labor supply curve   substitute input
marginal revenue product (MRP)   wage taker

CHAPTER HIGHLIGHTS

Fill in each blanks with the appropriate words or phrases. If you have difficulty, review the
chapter and then try again.

1. The demand sice of a labor market includes all firms hiring labor in that labor market.
   These firms may, but do not necessarily, compete in the same _____.

2. The demand for labor is a _____ demand—it arises from, and varies with,
   the demand for the firm's output.

3. In _____ labor markets, each firm is a _____: it takes
   the market wage as given.

4. The firm faces three constraints as it decides how much labor to employ: (1) Its
   _____ determines how much output the firm can produce with each
   quantity of labor; (2) the market _____ in its product market tells the firm
   how much it can sell its output for; and (3) the market _____ in its labor
   market tells the firm how much it must pay each worker.

5. The marginal revenue product (MRP) of labor is the change in _____
   from hiring another worker.

6. When output is sold in a competitive product market, the MRP can be calculated by
   multiplying the _____ by the price of output.

7. A firm should hire another worker whenever _____ is greater than _____, but not when _____ is less than _____.

8. To maximize profit, the firm should hire the number of workers such that _____ = _____, i.e., where the _____ curve intersects the _____ line.

9. When labor is the only variable input, the _____-sloping portion of the MRP curve is the firm's _____ curve, telling us how much labor the firm will want to employ at each _____.

10. Whether the firm can vary just labor, or several inputs simultaneously, the optimal level of employment will satisfy the _____ = _____ rule, and the firm's labor demand curve will slope _____: a decrease in the wage will cause a (an) _____ in employment.

11. The market labor demand curve tells us the total number of workers all firms in a labor market want to employ at each _____. It is found by horizontally _____ across all firms' individual labor demand curves.

12. The effect of a change in output price on labor demand depends on whether many firms in the labor market also share the same output market. When they do, a rise in output price will shift the market labor demand curve _____; a fall in output price will shift the market labor demand curve _____.

13. When many firms in the same labor market acquire a new technology, the market labor demand curve will shift rightward if the technology is _____ with (for) labor, and leftward if the technology is _____ with (for) labor.

14. When the price of some other input *decreases*, the market labor demand curve may shift rightward or leftward. It will shift rightward when that other input is _____ with (for) labor, and leftward when the other input is _____ with (for) labor.

15. In a competitive labor market, each seller is a _____; he or she takes the market wage rate as given.

16. The higher the wage rate, the greater the number of people whose reservation wages are exceeded, and the _____ the quantity of labor supplied.

17. A market labor supply curve will _____ when something other than a change in the wage rate causes a change in the number of people who want to work in a particular market.

18. As long as some individuals can choose to supply their labor in two different markets, a rise in the wage in one market will cause a _____ shift in the labor supply curve in the other market.

19. An increase in the cost of acquiring human capital needed to enter a labor market will shift the labor supply curve _____; a decrease in the cost of acquiring human capital will shift the labor supply curve _____.

20. The _____ tells us how many (qualified) people will want to work in a labor market at each wage rate, after all adjustments have taken place. Specifically, all those who want to _____ or who want to move to a new location have done so.

21. The long-run labor supply response is _____ wage elastic than the short-run labor supply response.

22. The forces of supply and demand will drive a competitive labor market to its _____ point—the point where the labor supply and labor demand curves _____.

23. In the short run, a shift in labor demand moves us along a short-run _____ curve. In the long run, the resulting change in the wage rate will cause entry or exit into the labor market, causing the short run _____ curve to shift as well.

24. Wage rates—like the prices of goods and services—act as _____— leading workers to move to areas where their work is most valued. When the labor demand curve shifts, the wage will _____ its long-run equilibrium value. But as the signal begins to work, the temporary _____ of the wage rate subsides.

25. Shortages and surpluses in a labor market are *not* the natural consequence of shifts in supply and demand curves. A labor _____ will occur only when the wage fails to rise to its equilibrium value. Similarly, a labor _____ will occur only when the wage fails to fall to its equilibrium value.

IMPORTANT CONCEPTS

Write a brief answer below each of the following questions.

1. List the three requirements of a perfectly competitive labor market.

   a.

   b.

   c.

2. Indicate whether this statement is true or false, and explain briefly: "In a competitive labor market, a firm must offer a higher wage in order to attract more workers."

3. When a firm's output is sold in a competitive market, there is a special formula for the calculation of the marginal revenue product. What is this formula?

4. List three different types of changes that would cause a market labor demand curve to shift *leftward* (Your textbook discusses four such changes.)

   a.

   b.

   c.

5. List three different types of changes that would cause a market labor supply curve to shift *rightward*. (Your textbook discusses four such changes.)

    a.

    b.

    c.

6. Suppose a new law were passed preventing people from moving from one location to another. How would the *long-run* labor supply curve be affected?

SKILLS AND TOOLS

For each of the following items, follow the instructions, write the correct answer in the blank, or circle the correct answer.

1. The owners of Collegeview Sandwich Shop are trying to decide how many student workers to employ in the short run. They have not been able to put together all the information they need, so the table below is incomplete.

Quantity of Labor	Total Product	Marginal Product of Labor (MPL)	Price per Sandwich	Total Revenue	Marginal Revenue Product (MRP)	Wage (W)
0	0		$4	$0		$50
		30			_____	
1	_____		4	_____		50
		_____			_____	
2	_____		4	_____		50
		30			_____	
3	100		4	_____		50
		20			_____	
4	_____		4	_____		50
		_____			$40	
5	_____		4	_____		50
		_____			_____	
6	120		4	_____		50

a. Complete the table for Collegeview's owners.

b. If these owners follow the marginal approach to profits when deciding whether to hire an additional worker, they will compare the (MPL/MRP) of the additional worker to the (price of a sandwich/wage/quantity of labor employed). If the former exceeds the latter, the firm will increase its profit by (hiring the additional worker/refusing to hire the additional worker/dismissing the last worker hired). If we apply this test to the data in the preceding table, will the owners of Collegeview hire the first worker? (Yes/No) Will they hire the second worker? (Yes/No) Will they hire the third worker? (Yes/No) How many workers will Collegeview employ? _____

2. It seems that the owners of the Collegeview Sandwich Shop have trouble interpreting data from tables—they prefer to use graphs instead.

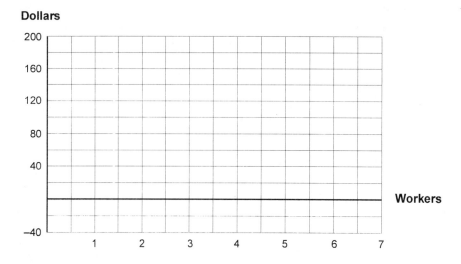

a. In the space provided, plot Collegeview's marginal revenue product (MRP) curve. (Remember to observe the convention of plotting values at the midpoint of the range over which they are computed.)

b. Using the graph, how many workers should Collegeview hire if

the wage is $100? _____

the wage is $60? _____

3. Only three firms produce oil lamps in the local market: Northern Lights, Major Electric, and Bright Lights. If you want to be an oil-lamp worker, you'll have to work for one of these firms, whose respective labor demand schedules are given below.

a. Plot each firm's labor demand curve in the space provided to the right of its demand schedule on the following page.

Northern Lights

Wage (W)	Number of Workers Demanded
$13	2
11	4
9	6
7	8
5	10
3	12
1	14

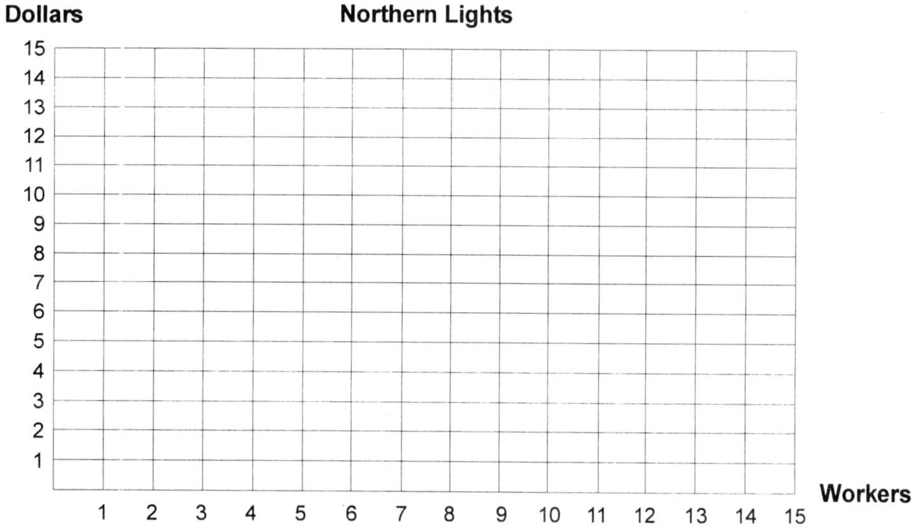

Dollars   **Northern Lights**

Workers

Major Electric

Wage (W)	Number of Workers Demanded
$13	1
11	2
9	3
7	4
5	5
3	6
1	7

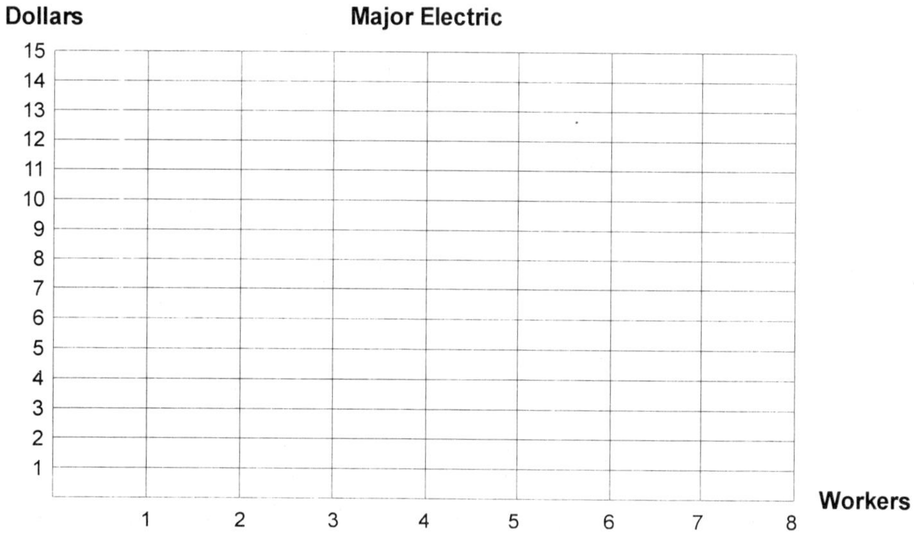

Dollars   **Major Electric**

Workers

Bright Lights

Wage (W)	Number of Workers Demanded
$13	4
11	8
9	12
7	16
5	20
3	24
1	28

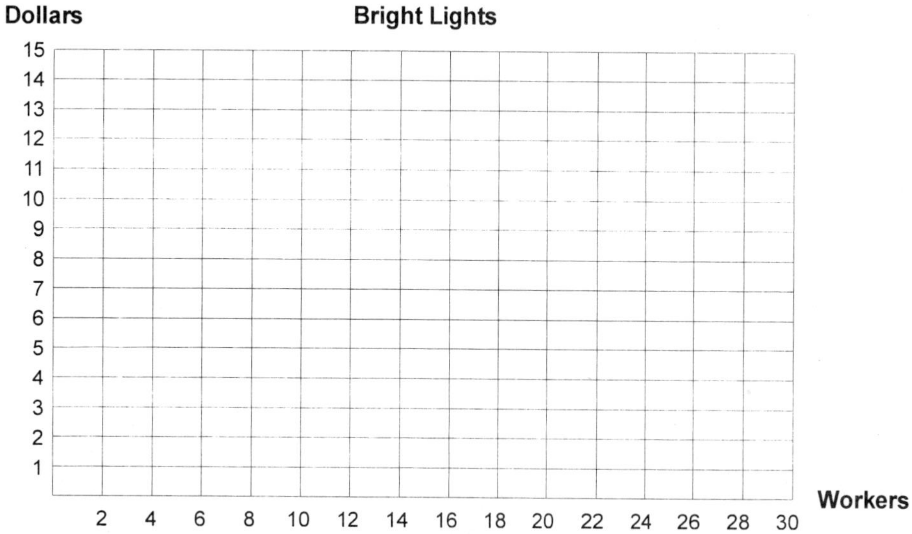

Dollars   **Bright Lights**

Workers

b. The United Lamp Workers' Union would like to determine the *market* demand for lamp
workers. Using the information above, graph that market labor demand curve on the grid
below.

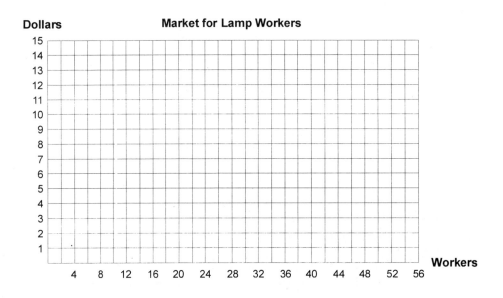

c. When the wage is $11, how many workers will be demanded in this labor market?
_____ How many of these will be demanded by Northern Lights?
_____ How many by Major Electric? _____ How many by
Bright Lights? _____

d. When the wage is $3, how many workers will be demanded in this labor market?
_____ How many of these will be demanded by Northern Lights?
_____ How many by Major Electric? _____ How many by
Bright Lights? _____

4. When financial research firms sell information abroad, they ordinarily translate the
information into the buyer's language. To perform that work, these firms routinely hire
translators. The following is the market labor supply curve for workers who can translate
English to Japanese.

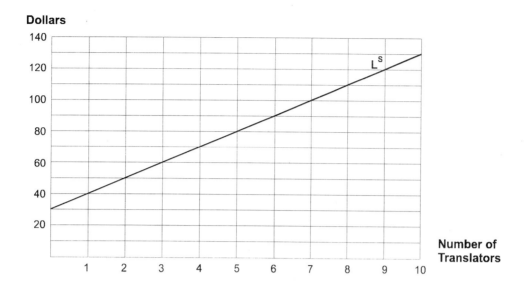

a. How many translators are willing to work at a wage of $50 per hour? _____ How many at a wage of $70? _____ An increase in the wage to as much as $100 per hour will (cause the labor supply curve to shift leftward/cause the labor supply curve to shift rightward/cause a movement along the labor supply curve).

b. Suppose the market demand curve for English/Japanese translators is given by:

$$L^D = 7 - W/40,$$

where W is the hourly wage and L^D is the number of translators demanded.

Plot the labor demand curve on the grid above. What is the equilibrium wage for translators? _____ How many translators will be employed? _____

5. Every spring, economic and management consulting firms across the United States hire thousands of new college graduates as economic analysts (EAs) and research assistants (RAs). Assume the labor market for EAs and RAs is perfectly competitive.

a. If market labor demand is given by the equation

$$L^D = 7,500 - 100W,$$

and market labor supply is given by the equation

$$L^S = 1000 + 160W,$$

what is the equilibrium market wage for EAs and RAs? _____ How many EAs and RAs will be hired this year? _____

b. Hoopers/Skybrand, a well-known consulting firm, has an office in Atlanta that hires new RAs and EAs every spring. The office has determined that the MRP for new EAs/RAs is given by the equation

$$MRP = 40 - L,$$

where L denotes the number of RAs and EAs it hires. If Hoopers/Skybrand must pay the market wage you determined in part (a), how many new EAs/RAs will the office hire this year? _____

6. Just about every farm in Titanic Valley grows iceberg lettuce—conditions there just seem perfect for it. Of course, many other farms outside the valley also grow lettuce, so Titanic's growers compete on the perfectly competitive national lettuce market.

At the current market price for iceberg lettuce, market labor demand for farm workers in the Valley is

$$L^D = 500 - 10W$$

where L^D is the number of workers hired per day and W is the daily wage.

In the short run, market labor supply in the Valley is

$$L^S = 20W - 100,$$

where L^S is the number of workers who offer their labor and W is the daily wage.

a. Plot market labor demand and short run market labor supply on the grid provided.

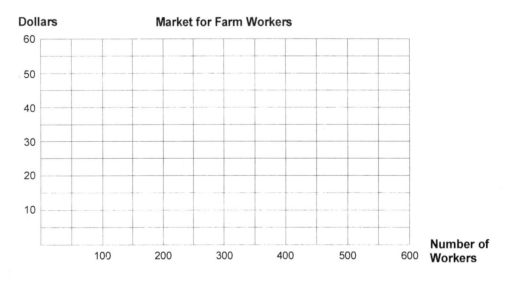

b. What is the equilibrium market wage for farm workers in the Valley? _____
What is the equilibrium level of employment in the short run? _____

c. Suppose the Lettuce Board's new promotional slogan *Lettuce Alone!* takes the country by storm, permanently increasing the demand for lettuce. In the short run, we would expect the market price of lettuce to (increase/decrease) as a result. Because the demand for farm workers in Titanic Valley is a derived demand, this (increase/decrease) in the price of lettuce will cause the market labor (demand curve/supply curve) for farm workers to shift (leftward/rightward).

d. Let us suppose that the shift in part (c) is in the amount of exactly 150 workers per day at every wage rate. Carefully draw in the new labor market (demand curve/supply curve) on the grid. What is the new short run equilibrium wage earned by farm workers in Titanic Valley? _____ What is the new short run equilibrium level of employment? _____

e. In the long run, we would expect the new (higher/lower) wages for farm workers in Titanic Valley to cause some workers to (move to/move away from) Titanic Valley and (seek employment/quit their employment). In the long run, after all adjustments have taken place, we would therefore expect the wage farm workers earn to be (higher/lower) than the wage we found in part (d), and we would expect the level of employment to be (higher/lower) than we found in part (d).

15-MINUTE PRACTICE TEST

Set a timer, giving yourself just 15 minutes to answer all of the following questions. To see what you *really* know and remember, take the test at least a day *after* you've read the chapter in the text and completed the exercises in this study guide.

Multiple Choice: Circle the letter in front of the single best answer.

1. Which of the following is *not* a requirement for a perfectly competitive labor market?
   a. All workers in the market have the same reservation wage.
   b. There are many buyers and sellers of labor.
   c. All workers in the market appear the same to firms.
   d. There are no barriers to entering the labor market.
   e. There are no barriers to leaving the labor market.

2. When labor is the only variable input for a firm in a competitive labor market, the firm should continue to hire additional workers as long as
   a. total revenue is greater than total cost.
   b. marginal product of labor is greater than the price of output.
   c. marginal revenue product of labor is greater than marginal revenue cost.
   d. the market wage rate is greater than the reservation wage.
   e. marginal revenue product of labor is greater than the wage rate.

3. When labor is the only variable input, the firm's labor demand curve is
    a. the entire MRP curve.
    b. the downward sloping portion of the MRP curve.
    c. the upward sloping portion of the MRP curve.
    d. a horizontal line at the market wage rate.
    e. a vertical line at the market wage rate.

4. If the price of output rises for many firms that hire their labor in the same labor market, then
    a. the market labor supply curve will shift rightward.
    b. the market labor supply curve will shift leftward.
    c. the market labor demand curve will shift rightward.
    d. the market labor demand curve will shift leftward.
    e. neither the market labor demand curve nor the market labor supply curve will shift.

5. When many firms in a labor market begin using a new input which is substitutable for labor,
    a. the market labor supply curve will shift rightward.
    b. the market labor supply curve will shift leftward.
    c. the market labor demand curve will shift rightward.
    d. the market labor demand curve will shift leftward.
    e. both the market labor demand curve and the market labor supply curve will shift rightward.

6. In a competitive labor market,
    a. firms are always wage takers, but workers are not.
    b. firms are sometimes wage takers, but workers are not.
    c. workers are always wage takers, but firms are not.
    d. both firms and workers are always wage takers.
    e. neither firms nor workers are wage takers.

7. Which of the following will shift the market labor supply curve leftward?
    a. A rise in the wage rate in some other labor market
    b. A rise in the cost of acquiring human capital needed in that labor market
    c. A decrease in population in that labor market
    d. All of the above
    e. None of the above

8. Which of the following would cause a firm's MRP curve to shift rightward?
    a. A decrease in the price of the firm's output
    b. A rise in the wage rate
    c. A fall in the wage rate
    d. An increase in population
    e. None of the above

9. In the long run, after a rightward shift in a market labor demand curve, we expect
   a. the market wage to be higher.
   b. the short-run labor supply curve to have shifted rightward.
   c. an increase in employment in the labor market.
   d. all of the above.
   e. none of the above.

10. If the market labor demand curve shifts *rightward*, then a
   a, labor shortage will generally occur.
   b. labor surplus will generally occur.
   c. labor shortage will occur only if the wage rate fails to rise to its new equilibrium value.
   d. labor shortage will occur only if the wage rate fails to drop to its new equilibrium value.
   e. labor surplus will occur only if the wage rate fails to drop to its new equilibrium value.

True/False: For each of the following statements, circle T if the statement is true or F if the statement is false.

T   F   1. The market labor demand curve is obtained by adding up the labor demand curves of all firms in the same output market.

T   F   2. If an individual's reservation wage for a particular labor market is $15 per hour, then firms will hire that individual only if they can pay a wage rate less than $15 per hour.

T   F   3. The long-run labor supply curve tells us the number of workers who want to work in a labor market at each wage rate after all those who want to move to a new location or acquire new job skills have done so.

T   F   4. As long as the firm operates in a competitive labor market, its MRP is given by the formula MRP = P × MPL.

T   F   5. In a competitive labor market, the optimal level of employment will satisfy the MRP = W rule, even if the firm can vary other inputs besides labor.

T   F   6. A government subsidy that lowers the cost of going to college will cause a rightward shift in the market demand curve for college-educated labor.

T   F   7. The long-run labor supply response is more wage elastic than the short-run labor supply response.

T   F   8. A change in tastes that decreases most peoples' reservation wages in a labor market will cause a rightward shift in the labor supply curve, and a decrease in the market wage.

CHAPTER 12

INCOME INEQUALITY

Fill in each blank with the appropriate word or phrase from the list provided in the word bank. (For a challenge, fill in as many blanks as you can *without* using the word bank.)

_____ 1. A difference in wage rates that makes two job equally attractive to a worker.

_____ 2. Any aspect of a job—other than the wage rate—that matters to a potential or current employee.

_____ 3. When a group of people have different opportunities because of personal characteristics that have nothing to do with their abilities.

_____ 4. When individuals are excluded from an activity based on the probability of behavior in their group, rather than their personal characteristics.

_____ 5. Income derived from supplying capital, land, or natural resources.

_____ 6. Any payment that is not compensation for supplying goods or services.

_____ 7. The percent of families whose incomes fall below a certain minimum.

_____ 8. The income level below which a family is considered in poverty.

_____ 9. When households are arrayed according to their incomes, a line showing the cumulative percent of income received by each cumulative percent of households.

_____ 10. A measure of income inequality; the ratio of the area above the Lorenz curve to the area under the diagonal.

Word Bank

compensating wage differential   poverty line
discrimination   poverty rate
Gini coefficient   property income
Lorenz curve   statistical discrimination
nonmonetary job characteristic   transfer payment

CHAPTER HIGHLIGHTS

Fill in the blanks with the appropriate word or phrase. If you have difficulty, review the chapter and then try again.

1. A _____ wage differential is the difference in wage rates that makes two jobs _____ to a worker.

2. The _____ characteristics of different jobs give rise to _____ wage differentials. Jobs considered intrinsically less attractive will tend to pay _____ wages, other things equal.

3. Differences in living costs can cause _____ wage differentials. Areas where living costs are _____ than average will tend to have higher-than-average wages.

4. Differences in _____ capital requirements can give rise to _____ wage differentials. Jobs that require more costly training will tend to pay _____ wage rates, other things equal.

5. In general, those with greater talent, intelligence, or perseverance will be more productive on the job and generate more revenue for firms. Thus, firms will be willing to pay them a _____ wage.

6. Through a (an) _____ in member wages and a (an) _____ in nonmember wages, unions create a wage differential between union and nonunion labor markets.

7. When prejudice originates with _____, market forces work to discourage discrimination and reduce or eliminate any wage gap between the favored and the unfavored group.

8. When prejudice originates with _____ or _____, market forces encourage, rather than discourage, discrimination and can lead to a permanent wage gap between the favored and unfavored group.

9. In measuring the impact of job-market discrimination on earnings, the wage gap between two groups gives an _____-estimate, since it fails to account for differences in skills and experience. However, comparing only workers with similar skills and experience leads to an _____-estimate, since some of the differences are themselves caused by discrimination—both in the job market and outside of it.

10. The larger the Gini coefficient—up to a maximum of _____ —the _____ is the degree of income inequality.

11. Poverty has been far from a lifetime sentence for the majority of the American poor. But for a small minority, poverty is a stubborn problem. All of this information is hidden by the simple _____ itself.

12. Inequality that results from choices that any of us can make is generally regarded as _____.

IMPORTANT CONCEPTS

Write a brief answer below each of the following questions.

1. List three explanations for compensating wage differentials.

   a.

   b.

   c.

2. List three explanations, *aside from* compensating wage differentials, for differences in wages among jobs.

   a.

   b.

   c.

3. List three different groups whose prejudice could cause wage discrimination. In each case, do market forces encourage or discourage the discrimination?

    a.

    b.

    c.

4. The text points out that a failure to distinguish between "earned income" and "available income" can distort our measures of inequality. List *three* differences between these two measures of income. In each case, explain whether the difference leads to an overestimate or underestimate of income inequality.

    a.

    b.

    c.

5. The minimum wage affects three different groups of workers. List the three groups, and, for each group, explain the impact of an increase in the minimum wage on the wage rate and employment.

    a.

    b.

    c.

SKILLS AND TOOLS

For each of the following items, follow the instructions, write the correct answer in the blank, or circle the correct answer.

1. Residents on the island of Harmony are either Reds or Greens. There are only two industries on the island—Hunting and Gathering. It is well known that Greens and Reds are equally

qualified to work in Hunting or Gathering. There are 15 Reds on the island, and no matter what the wage is all 15 will want to work. There are 40 Greens on the island, and no matter what the wage is all 40 will want to work. Letting L^D and L^S stand for the number of workers demanded and supplied at wage W, respectively, we know the following additional facts about labor supply and labor demand on the island:

Market Labor Demand in the Hunting Industry: $L^D_H = 30 - W$
Market Labor Demand in the Gathering Industry: $L^D_G = 50 - W$
Labor Supply of all Reds combined: $L^S_R = 15$
Labor Supply of all Greens combined: $L^S_G = 40$

a. Suppose that because of employer prejudice, Hunter firms will hire only Reds, and Gatherer firms will hire only Greens. What is the equilibrium wage earned by Red workers? _____ What is the equilibrium wage earned by Green workers? _____

b. Suppose that attitudes change overnight and employers stop discriminating: Firms in either industry are now equally willing to hire Greens and Reds to work for them. Once the labor market in Harmony reaches its new equilibrium, we know that the wage paid to any Red working in the Hunter industry will be (higher than/the same as/lower than) the wage paid to any Green working in the Hunter industry. Similarly, the wage paid to any Red working in the Gatherer industry will be (higher than/the same as/lower than) the wage paid to any Green working in the Gatherer industry. Moreover, we know that the wage paid in the Hunter industry must be (higher than/the same as/less than) the wage paid in the Gatherer industry . If this were not so, workers would move from the (higher wage industry/lower wage industry) to the (higher wage industry/lower wage industry). Then is the following statement true or false? "In the new equilibrium, every worker— Red or Green—must earn the same wage, no matter which industry employs that worker." (True/False)

c. If, as in (b), employers no longer discriminate between Reds and Greens, what wage will a Green earn in the final labor market equilibrium?_____ What wage will a Red earn? _____ (Try to work this out on your own, but if you get stuck, there is a hint in the answers section.)

d. Most people think we'd all be better off if no one were prejudiced against anyone else. To see if that is true in Harmony, compare your answers in (a) to your answers in (c). The typical Red worker is (better off/worse off) when there is employer prejudice. The typical Green worker is (better off/worse off) when there is employer prejudice. Does everyone gain from eliminating employer prejudice? (Yes/No)

2. Your text reports the following data on the distribution of income in the United States from the *Historical Income Tables, 1967-98:*

**Percent of Total Household Income Earned by
Each Fifth of U.S. Households**

	Lowest Fifth	Second Fifth	Third Fifth	Fourth Fifth	Highest Fifth
1970	4.1%	10.8%	17.1%	24.5%	43.3%
1998	3.6%	9.0%	15.0%	23.2%	49.2%

a. Using this data, plot the U.S. Lorenz curves in each of the two years 1970 and 1998. Be sure to label the axes properly, and draw in the line of complete equality.

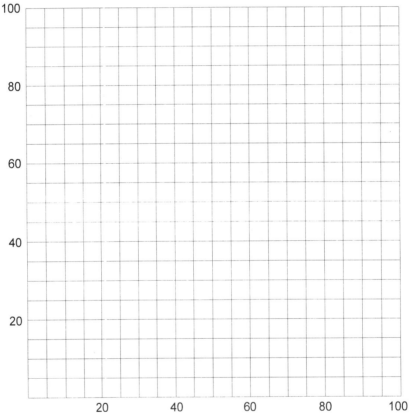

b. We can see that the Lorenz curve for 1998 is (more/less) bowed out in the middle than the Lorenz curve for 1970. From this we conclude that income inequality in the United States (increased/decreased) over the twenty-eight years between between 1970 and 1998.

3. In this problem, you will construct a Lorenz curve from scratch to get a better feel for how it is done. Suppose there are just ten families in society, Families A through J. Their annual family incomes are reported in the following table.

Family	Income
A	$40,000
B	27,000
C	40,000
D	18,000
E	6,000
F	13,000
G	4,000
H	8,000
I	27,000
J	27,000

Total Income _____

a. Compute total annual income in this society and report it in the blank provided in the table above.

b. Make the necessary computations and complete the entries in the table below.

   Hints: (1) With ten families in all, each family is 10% of the total number of families.

   (2) "Percent of income" is the family's income as a percent of the total income in society.

Family	Percent of Population	Cumulative Percent of Population	Ordered Income (Lowest to (Highest)	Percent of Income	Cumulative Percent of Income
_____	10%	10%	_____	2%	_____
_____	_____	_____	_____	_____	5%
_____	_____	_____	_____	_____	_____
_____	_____	_____	$13,000	_____	_____
D	_____	_____	_____	_____	_____
_____	_____	60%	_____	13%	_____
_____	_____	_____	_____	13%	49%
_____	_____	_____	_____	_____	_____
_____	_____	_____	_____	_____	_____
_____	_____	100%	_____	_____	100%

c. Suppose it costs $3,000 per year to feed a person in this society, and suppose there are exactly *three* people in every family. Using the definition in the text, what is the poverty line in this society? _____ How many families live below the poverty line? _____ What is the poverty rate? _____

d. Plot the Lorenz curve for this society in the grid provided.

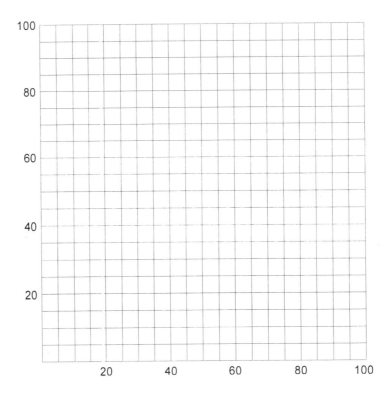

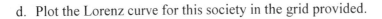

15-MINUTE PRACTICE TEST

Set a timer, giving yourself just 15 minutes to answer all of the following questions. To see what you *really* know and remember, take the test at least a day *after* you've read the chapter in the text and completed the exercises in this study guide.

Multiple Choice: Circle the letter in front of the single best answer.

1. Under three assumptions, all workers would earn *identical* wages in the long run. Which of the following is *one* of these assumptions?
   a. All workers are properly compensated for human capital investments.
   b. Except for differences in wages, all jobs are equally attractive to all workers.
   c. All jobs pay an appropriate compensating differential.
   d. All of the above.
   e. None of the above.

2. Which of the following typically results in a compensating wage differential?
   a. Nonmonetary job characteristics
   b. Barriers to entry
   c. Statistical discrimination
   d. All of the above
   e. None of the above

3. Cost-of-living differences that lead to differences in wages in different cities are an example of

   a. non-monetary job characteristics.
   b. compensating wage differentials.
   c. barriers to entry.
   d. statistical discrimination.
   e. none of the above.

4. Discrimination occurs when a difference in wages is due to

   a. compensating wage differentials.
   b. non-monetary job characteristics.
   c. differences in ability.
   d. all of the above.
   e. none of the above.

5. Market forces work to discourage discrimination and reduce any wage gap when the discrimination arises from prejudice by

   a. employers.
   b. employees.
   c. customers.
   d. all of the above.
   e. none of the above.

6. The poverty line for a U.S. family of a certain size is equal to

   a. what it would cost to feed that family.
   b. what it would cost to feed and clothe that family.
   c. about triple what it would cost to feed that family.
   d. the income needed to reach the bottom 10 percent of the U.S. income distribution.
   e. what the average income level for that family was twenty years earlier.

7. A Gini coefficient is a measure of income inequality derived from

   a. the poverty rate.
   b. income mobility studies.
   c. the Lorenz curve.
   d. all of the above.
   e. none of the above.

8. When income changes over time are taken into account,

   a. income inequality increases substantially.
   b. income inequality is unchanged.
   c. income inequality is lessened.
   d. almost all of the income inequality in the United States disappears.
   e. we discover that the poverty line is a better measure of income inequality than the Lorenz curve.

9. Most people seem to agree that income inequality due to _____ is entirely fair.

    a. statistical discrimination
    b. inherited wealth
    c. difference in wages
    d. differences in non-wage income
    e. compensating wage differentials

10. A higher minimum wage can be expected to cause

    a. higher wages for skilled workers.
    b. higher employment for skilled workers.
    c. lower wages for *un*skilled workers *not* covered by the minimum wage.
    d. all of the above.
    e. none of the above.

True/False: For each of the following statements, circle T if the statement is true or F if the statement is false.

T   F   1. Jobs that require greater abilities or talents virtually always pay more than jobs that are easier and that more people can do.

T   F   2. If we compare the wages of two groups, such as whites and blacks, and we limit ourselves to workers with similar skills and experience, the measured wage gap will underestimate the total effect of discrimination on wages.

T   F   3. The Lorenz curve for U.S. *wealth* shows greater inequality than the Lorenz curve for U.S. *income*.

T   F   4. According to a simple supply and demand model, unions not only raise the wages of union members, they also cause the wages of non-union members to decrease.

T   F   5. Statistical discrimination occurs when an employer refuses to hire members of a certain group because of prejudice against that group.

T   F   6. The larger the Gini coefficient, the greater the degree of income inequality.

T   F   7. From year to year, most countries experience large changes in their Gini coefficients.

T   F   8. As a group, unskilled workers who are *not* covered by minimum wage legislation benefit from a higher minimum wage.

CHAPTER 13

CAPITAL AND FINANCIAL MARKETS

Fill in each blank with the appropriate word or phrase from the list provided in the word bank.
(For a challenge, fill in as many blanks as you can *without* using the word bank.)

_____ 1. The increase in revenue from a one-unit increase in capital.

_____ 2. What a sum of money to be received in the future is worth in today's dollars.

_____ 3. The act of converting a future value into its present-day equivalent.

_____ 4. The interest rate used in computing present values.

_____ 5. The idea that the value of an asset is equal to the total present value of all the future benefits it generates. .

_____ 6. Knowledge, education, or training that is valuable at many different firms.

_____ 7. Knowledge, education or training that is valuable only at a specific firm.

_____ 8. A promise to pay future income in some form, such as future dividends or future interest payments.

_____ 9. A promise to pay a specific sum of money at some future date.

_____ 10. The amount of money a bond promises to pay when it matures.

_____ 11. The day that a bond's principal will be paid to the bond's owner.

_____ 12. A bond that promises no payments except for the principal it pays at maturity.

_____ 13. A series of periodic payments that a bond promises before maturity.

_____ 14. The rate of return a bond earns for its owner.

_____ 15. Where newly issued financial assets are sold for the first time.

_____ 16. Where previously issued financial assets are sold.

_____ 17. A share of ownership in a corporation.

_____ 18. A corporation that specializes in owning shares of stock in other corporations.

_____ 19. The part of a firm's current profit distributed to shareholders.

_____ 20. The return someone gets by selling a financial asset at a price higher than they paid for it.

_____ 21. An index of the prices of stocks of 30 large U.S. firms.

_____ 22. An index of the prices of stocks of 500 large corporations.

_____ 23. A method of predicting a stock's price based on the forces driving the firm's future earnings.

_____ 24. A method of predicting a stock's price based on that stock's past behavior.

_____ 25. A market that instantaneously incorporates all available information relevant to a stock's price.

Word Bank

bond	mutual fund
capital gain	present value
coupon payment	primary markets
discount rate	principal (face value)
discounting	principle of asset valuation
dividend	pure discount bond
Dow Jones industrial average	secondary market
efficient markets	share of stock
financial asset	specific human capital
fundamental analysis	Standard & Poor's 500
general human capital	technical analysis
marginal revenue product of capital	yield
maturity date	

CHAPTER HIGHLIGHTS

Fill in the blanks with the appropriate word or phrase. If you have difficulty, review the chapter and then try again.

1. Because present dollars can earn _____ , and because _____ must be paid to borrow present dollars, it is always preferable to receive the same sum of money earlier rather than later. Therefore, a dollar received now is worth _____ than a dollar received later.

2. The *present value* of a future payment is the value of that future payment in _____ dollars. Alternatively, it is the most anyone would pay today for the right to receive the future payment.

3. The present value of $Y to be received n years in the future is equal to (give the formula): _____

4. The present value of a future payment is smaller if (1) the size of the payment itself is smaller; (2) the interest rate is _____ ; or (3) the payment is received _____ .

5. The principal of asset valuation says that the value of any asset is the sum of the _____ of all the future benefits it generates.

6. As the interest rate _____ , each business firm in the economy—using the principal of asset valuation—will place a lower value on additional capital, and decide to purchase less of it. Therefore, in the economy as a whole, a _____ in the interest rate causes a decrease in investment expenditures.

7. _____ interest rates increase firms' investment in physical capital, causing the capital stock to be larger, and our overall standard of living to be _____ .

8. Employers have limited incentives to provide _____ human capital, since it increases the worker's value to many firms, and the worker will capture the benefits in the form of a higher wage. Therfore, workers must acquire _____ human capital on their own—or with the help of government subsidies.

9. Individuals have little incentive to pay for _____ human capital, since it increases their value to only one firm, and that firm will capture the benefits. Therefore, firms provide their workers with _____ human capital at the firm's expense.

10. The benefit of any given human capital investment to a worker is equal to the total
    _____ of the additional future income that the worker will earn from the
    investment.

11. Investment in human capital, like investment in _____ capital, is
    _____ related to the interest rate. The lower the interest rate, the
    _____ the benefits of any human capital investment, and the
    _____ human capital workers will want to acquire.

12. _____ interest rates encourage individuals to invest in general human
    capital. As a result, the total amount of human capital—and our overall standard of living—
    will be higher if interest rates are _____ .

13. There is an inverse relationship between bond _____ and bond yields.
    The higher the _____ of any given bond, the lower the yield on that
    bond.

14. If a bond's price rises in the secondary market, the price one can charge for similar, newly
    issued bonds in the _____ market will rise as well.

15. To put a value on riskier bonds, market participants use a _____ discount
    rate than on safe bonds. This leads to _____ total present values and
    _____ prices for the riskier bonds. With _____
    prices, riskier bonds have _____ yields.

16. The value of a share of stock in a firm is equal to the total _____ of the
    firm's after-tax profits divided by _____ .

17. The following will each *increase* the value of a share of stock: a (an)
    _____ in current profits; a (an) _____ in the
    anticipated growth rate of profits; a (an) _____ in interest rates; an
    anticipated _____ in interest rates; and a (an) _____
    in the perceived riskiness of future profits.

18. According to the efficient markets view, neither _____ analysis nor
    _____ analysis can help anyone outperform the market.

IMPORTANT CONCEPTS

Write a brief answer below each of the following questions.

1. Briefly, what is the difference between general human capital and specific human capital? Who typically pays for the acquisition of general human capital—the worker or the firm? Who typically pays for the acquisition of specific human capital?

2. True or false, and explain briefly: "The higher the interest rate or yield on a bond, the more it is worth, so the higher will be its price."

3. Briefly explain why the economy's investment curve slopes downward.

4. The text discusses four contributions of financial markets to the functioning of the economy. List them.

a.

b.

c.

d.

SKILLS AND TOOLS

For each of the following items, follow the instructions, write the correct answer in the blank, or circle the correct answer.

1. Your text explains how to compute present value. For practice, and because it will be useful for reference in subsequent problems, complete the table below, which reports the present value of $1 to be received at different points in the future, given various prevailing rates of interest (Remember to check your answers in the back of the book before you go on to the next question.)

PV of $1 received *n* years in the future, given interest rate *i*

		Years (*n*)					
		1	2	3	4	5	20
	5%	___	___	___	0.82	0.78	0.38
Interest Rate	10%	___	0.83	___	0.68	0.62	0.15
(*i*)	15%	___	___	0.66	0.57	0.50	0.06
	20%	___	___	___	0.48	___	0.03

2.   Most state lotteries advertise the Big Jackpot with great fanfare. Who wouldn't want a chance to win millions of dollars? But just how much is a million-dollar jackpot worth? The answer can depend very much on two things: (1) the rate of interest and, (2) just how the jackpot is to be paid out.

   a.   Assume the interest rate at which you can borrow or lend is 5% per annum. What is the present value of a $2 million jackpot if it is paid in one single payment on the following dates:

   today _____

   one year from today _____

   two years from today_____

   five years from today _____

   twenty years from today _____

   b.   Assume the interest rate at which you can borrow or lend is 15% per annum. What is the present value of a $2 million jackpot if it is paid in one single payment on the following dates:

   today _____

   one year from today _____

   two years from today_____

   five years from today _____

   twenty years from today _____

   c.   Lotteries usually do not pay out the jackpot all at once. Instead, they normally spread the payments over a number of years. If the interest rate is 15% per annum, what is the present value of a $2 million jackpot if it is paid out in five equal annual payments starting today? _____

   d.   *Challenge:* What is the present value of this $2 million jackpot if the interest rate is 15%, but the payout (as is typical) is in twenty equal annual payments starting today? _____ (Note: You *cannot* use the preceding table to solve this one. Use your calculator, a spreadsheet or look up a more extensive present value table in a finance text.)

3. Four web-savvy friends—Azfar, Rashida, Mike and Zoey—have a great deal of free time now that they are in college. As a result, they've decided to open a student travel agency on the Internet and run it out of the dorm part-time. They've got the Internet access for free (until the computer center catches on) , but they'll need some computers. They all agree they will set up their first computer as a server—the core of their whole business—where they'll mount their web site, booking and billing software, etc.. If they get a second one, they could use it to search the web for special travel deals and to book the tours and airline reservations for their call-in clients. They know that customer support can be critical, so if they got a third machine they would devote it to customer support, using it to process client e-mail, log phone messages and generally build the client database. They don't want to forget about advertising, so if they get a fourth machine, they would devote that one to spamming the campus with their ads on a regular basis.

With technology changing so quickly, they know that any machine they buy today will have to be junked and replaced in three (**3**) years time. The friends have estimated the additional revenue each successive machine would contribute to their business each year, and recorded it in the table below.

Computer	Additional Annual Revenue	Total Present Value with a discount rate of:	
		5%	**10%**
1	$8,000	_____	_____
2	$5,000	_____	_____
3	$2,000	_____	_____
4	$1,000	_____	_____

a. Using the present value table you computed in question (1), and assuming a discount rate of **5%**, we can see that the additional annual revenue (MRP_K) generated by the *first* machine in the *first* year of its useful life has a present value of _____ dollars. The MRP_K of the first machine in the *second* year of its useful life has a (greater/smaller) present value of _____ dollars. The MRP_K of the first machine in the *third* (and final) year of its useful life has an even (greater/smaller) present value of _____ dollars. With a three-year useful life, and using a discount rate of 5%, the total present value of the additional revenue generated by the first computer these friends buy is _____ dollars.

b. The friends are not so sure 5% is the best discount rate for them to use. If, instead, they decide to use a discount rate of **10%** , we can see that the additional annual revenue (MRP_K) generated by the *first* machine in the *first* year of its useful life has a present value of _____ dollars. The MRP_K of the first machine in the *second* year of its useful life has a (greater/smaller) present value of _____ dollars. The MRP_K of the first machine in the *third* (and final) year of its useful life has an even (greater/smaller) present value of _____ dollars. With a three-year useful life, and using a discount rate of 10%, the total present value of the additional revenue generated by the first computer purchased is _____ dollars.

c. Record the total present values you calculated in parts (a) and (b) in the table above. Then complete the table.

d. The computers they want cost $5,000 each, fully loaded. If these friends decide to use a discount rate of 5%, they should (definitely/definitely not) buy the first machine, because the present value of the additional revenue it will generate over its useful life (exceeds/falls short of) its cost. They should (definitely/definitely not) buy the second machine, because the present value of the additional revenue it will generate over its useful life (exceeds/falls short of) its cost. They should (definitely/definitely not) buy the third machine, because the present value of the additional revenue it will generate over its useful life (exceeds/falls short of) its cost. They should (definitely/definitely not) buy the fourth machine, because the present value of the additional revenue it will generate over its useful life (exceeds/falls short of) its cost. Thus, with a discount rate of 5%, and at a cost of $5,000 per machine, a total of _____ should be purchased.

e. If they decide to use a discount rate of 10%, instead, then at a price of $5,000 per computer, these friends should (buy/ not buy) the first machine; they should (buy/ not buy) the second machine; they should (buy/ not buy) the third machine; and they should (buy/ not buy) the fourth machine. Thus, with a discount rate of 10%, a total of _____ computers should be purchased.

f. Comparing the results in parts (d) and (e), we can see that, other things equal, the higher the discount rate applied, the (fewer/more) machines that should be purchased.

4. Thanks to hard work and smart investment spending, the student travel business in the previous problem is booming. So much so that our friends are planning to sell some bonds to raise money so they can expand. They've decided they need to raise about $20,000. So that other students can afford them, they want to issue bonds with a face value of only $1,000, and no coupon payments. They plan to pay off their bonds in a single payment just before they graduate, so they've set the maturity date for each bond to be exactly four **(4)** years from now. Use the present value table in question (1) to answer the following questions.

   a. If the interest rate is 5%, each $1,000 bond has a present value of _____
dollars. The highest price anyone would pay for this bond is therefore _____
dollars. Thus, in order to raise about $20,000, they would have to sell approximately
_____ bonds at this price.

   b. If the interest rate is 10%, each $1,000 bond has a present value of _____
dollars. The highest price anyone would pay for this bond is therefore _____
dollars. Thus, in order to raise about $20,000, they would have to sell approximately
_____ bonds at this price.

5. Well, its been an amazing four years—the student travel business just took off and kept going.
Azfar, Rashida, Mike and Zoey not only learned a lot in their classes, they're set to become
millionaires, too—that is, if all goes well in the initial public offering (IPO) of stock in their
Internet start-up. In their final meeting with the investment bankers they just want to go over
the figures one more time.

   a. The Wall Street "suits" estimate that the firm will earn after-tax profits of $2 million each
year, forever, no sweat. If the discount rate is 5%, the present value of those future profits is
_____ dollars. Since the bankers have recommended that 500,000 shares in all
be issued, each share will have a value of _____ dollars.

   b. Azfar's not so sure, though. He thinks the profit forecasts are too high. If he's right, and the
market agrees with him, the value of the stock will be (higher than /the same as/lower than)
what the bankers have estimated in part (a).

   c. Rashida's not worried about the forecasts—she thinks they are right on target. She's worried
about interest rates. She thinks that interest rates are going to rise and—more importantly—
she thinks everyone in the market thinks so, too. If Rashida is right, the value of the stock
will be (higher than /the same as/lower than) what the bankers have estimated in part (a).

   d. Zoey thinks the other two are crazy. She sees nothing but good times ahead—in fact, she
expects profits to actually grow year after year, easily beating the bankers' $2 million dollar
per year estimate. If she is right, and if the market thinks the same way she does, the value
of the stock will be (higher than /the same as/lower than) what the bankers have estimated
in part (a).

15-MINUTE PRACTICE TEST

Set a timer, giving yourself just 15 minutes to answer all of the following questions. To see what you *really* know and remember, take the test at least a day *after* you've read the chapter in the text and completed the exercises in this study guide.

Multiple Choice: Circle the letter in front of the single best answer.

1. A firm's additional revenue from hiring one more unit of capital is called
   a. marginal revenue.
   b. marginal cost.
   c. the marginal product of capital.
   d. the marginal revenue product of capital.
   e. discounted capital.

2. Which of the following changes will *decrease* the present value of a future payment?
   a. The payment will be received earlier.
   b. The interest rate is higher.
   c. The payment will be received with greater certainty.
   d. All of the above
   e. None of the above

3. If the interest rate is 12%, then the present value of $100 to be received two years in the future is
   a. $144.
   b. $112.
   c. $89.29.
   d. $79.72.
   e. $69.44.

4. Consider the following three income streams A, B and C, each with three payments to be received at the end of 2002, 2003 and 2004, respectively:

YEAR	STREAM A	STREAM B	STREAM C
2002	$1,100	$900	$1,000
2003	$1,000	$1,000	$1,000
2004	$900	$1,100	$1,000

   For any interest rate larger than zero, if we rank the total present value of these streams from *lowest* to *highest*, we find:

   a. A < B < C.
   b. B < A < C.
   c. C < B < A.
   d. C < A < B
   e. B < C < A.

5. In general, if you expect interest rates to decrease, you should also expect
   a. stock prices to decrease.
   b. bond prices to increase.
   c. investment in physical capital to decrease.
   d. investment in human capital to decrease.
   e. all of the above.

6. Which of the following is an example of general human capital?
   a. a pilot's knowledge of different planes and how to fly them.
   b. a waiter's knowledge of which of a restaurant's customers are temperamental and which are not.
   c. a college professor's knowledge of different classrooms at the college, and knowledge of where in the college bureaucracy to request a good classroom.
   d. all of the above.
   e. none of the above.

7. A pure discount bond is one that
   a. is sold for less than its market price.
   b. has no coupon payments.
   c. has no maturity date.
   d. has no principal (face value).
   e. has a yield less than the yield on other, similar bonds.

8. The primary bond market is where
   a. the bonds of large corporations are bought and sold.
   b. the bonds of large corporations or the government are bought and sold.
   c. the bonds of small corporations only are bought and sold.
   d. newly issued bonds are sold for the first time.
   e. most of the day to day trading in previously issued bonds takes place.

9. According to the principal of asset valuation, the value of a share of stock in a corporation is equal to
   a. the value of one of its bonds.
   b. the total present value of its after-tax profits.
   c. the total present value of its after tax profits divided by the number of shares outstanding.
   d. the total present value of its retained earnings divided by the number of shares outstanding.
   e. the total present value of its retained earnings divided by the total present value of its dividends.

10. "You should buy XYZ stock right away. It's gone up at least 3 percent every week for the last 10 weeks, and it's *hot!*" This statement would most likely be made by a believer in
    a. fundamental analysis.
    b. technical analysis.
    c. efficient markets theory.
    d. the principle of asset valuation.
    e. the marginal revenue product of capital.

True/False: For each of the following statements, circle T if the statement is true or F if the statement is false.

T   F   1. The higher the interest rate, the greater the present value of any given future payment.

T   F   2. The principal of asset valuation says that the value of any asset is the simple sum of all the future benefits (e.g. future payments) that it generates.

T   F   3. Higher interest rates lead to lower levels of investment in both physical and human capital.

T   F   4. Specific human capital is typically paid for by the firm, while general human capital is typically paid for by workers themselves.

T   F   5. A rise in the interest rate will decrease bond prices in the primary market, but not in the secondary market.

T   F   6. All else equal, a riskier bond will earn a higher interest rate (yield) than a bond with less risk.

T   F   7. If a public offering of shares shifts the supply curve for a stock significantly rightward, we can expect the price of the stock to rise.

T   F   8. Economists who believe in efficient markets theory believe that only those with a high level of training in economics can predict stock prices well enough to outperform the general market.

CHAPTER 14

ECONOMIC EFFICIENCY AND THE COMPETITIVE IDEAL

SPEAKING ECONOMICS

Fill in each blank with the appropriate word or phrase from the list provided in the word bank. (For a challenge, fill in as many blanks as you can *without* using the word bank.)

Pareto improvement 1. An action that makes at least one person better off, and harms no one.

economic eff. 2. A situation in which every Pareto improvement has occurred.

productive eff. 3. When it is impossible to produce more of one good without producing less of some other good.

allocative eff. 4. When there is no change in quantity consumed of any good by any consumer that would be a Pareto improvement.

Word Bank

allocative efficiency
economic efficiency

Pareto improvement
productive efficiency

CHAPTER HIGHLIGHTS

Fill in the blanks with the appropriate words or phrases. If you have difficulty, review the chapter and then try again.

1. _____ is achieved when there is no way to rearrange the production or allocation of goods in a way that makes one person better off without making anybody worse off.

2. An efficient economy is not necessarily a _____ economy.

175

3. A Pareto improvement is any action that makes at least one person _____, and _____ .

4. Economic efficiency is achieved when every possible _____ has been exploited.

5. Some actions that—by themselves—would not be Pareto improvements can be converted into Pareto improvements if accompanied by an appropriate _____ .

6. An economy is _____ efficient when it is impossible to produce more of one good without producing less of some other good.

7. To be _____efficient, the overall economy must be operating at full employment, making use of all resources offered by resource owners.

8. _____efficiency requires that every firm in the economy produce the maximum possible output from the resources it is using.

9. _____ efficiency requires that resources be _____ among firms in such a way that the economy cannot increase the production of one good without decreasing the production of some other good.

10. _____markets tend to be productively efficient.

11. An economy in which firms are free to seek the maximum _____— whether markets are _____ or not—will tend to have full employment of resources.

12. Productive efficiency is necessary for _____ efficiency.

13. An economy is _____ efficient when there is no change in the quantity consumed of any good by any consumer that would be a _____ improvement.

14. The height of the _____ at any quantity shows us the marginal benefit—to someone—of the last unit of the good consumed.

15. The height of the _____ at any quantity measures the marginal cost—to some firm—of the last unit produced.

16. The efficient level of production of any good is where the marginal _____ and marginal _____ of the good are equal.

17. In perfectly competitive markets, the efficient quantity of a good—where marginal _____ and _____ are equal—is also the _____ quantity—where the supply and demand curves intersect.

18. Perfectly competitive markets tend to be economically efficient—that is, both _____ and _____ efficient.

19. In an imperfectly competitive market, the equilibrium price exceeds the firm's_____.

20. Monopoly and _____ markets, in which firms charge a price _____ than marginal cost, produce too _____ output at too _____ a price.

21. In monopoly and _____ markets, it is the inability of firms to make separate side deals through _____ that prevents _____ from being carried out.

IMPORTANT CONCEPTS

Write a brief answer below each of the following questions.

1. State whether each of the following would be a Pareto improvement or not.

   a. You pay a cleaning service $50 to clean your apartment.

   b. You and the apartment dweller next door strike a deal in which you will pay him $100 if he will turn down the volume on his TV until your lease is up.

   c. You would be willing to pay $200 per month in additional rent to live in a quiet neighborhood rather than a noisy one. One day, a disco opens up across the street, turning your neighborhood into a noisy one. The disco makes a profit of $1,000 per month. You try to move to a quiet neighborhood, but you are unsuccessful, so you stay and tolerate the noise.

2. Briefly, how do we know that an imperfectly competitive market does not produce the economically efficient quantity of a good? (Hint: Use price and marginal cost in your answer.)

3. List the three requirements for productive efficiency.

   a.

   b.

   c.

4. Indicate whether the following statement is true or false, and explain briefly. "Economic efficiency is necessary for productive efficiency."

5. The marginal product of labor in Firm A is 5, while the marginal product of labor in Firm B is 3. Both firms produce the same output. Is the economy productively efficient? Prove your answer.

6. Each of the following is an example of productive or allocative inefficiency. State which in each case.

   a. An economy is operating inside its PPF. _____

   b. An economy is operating *on* its PPF, but all consumers could be made better off if the economy were operating at a different point along the PPF. _____

   c. A car manufacturer is not producing the maximum possible output of automobiles from the land, labor, capital and natural resources it is using. _____

SKILLS AND TOOLS

For each of the following items, follow the instructions, write the correct answer in the blank, or circle the correct answer.

1. The New Orleans wholesale market for frozen medium shrimp is perfectly competitive. The weekly market supply curve and market demand curve are displayed below.

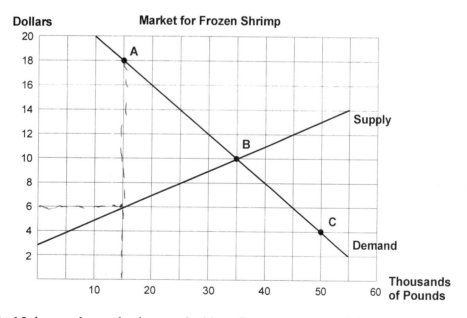

   a. At 15 thousand pounds, the marginal benefit to some buyer of the last thousand pounds of shrimp purchased is _____$18_____. The marginal cost of producing it at some firm is _____$6_____. Because marginal benefit is (greater than/equal to/less than) marginal cost, we can deduce that 15 thousand pounds (is/is not) the economically efficient level of production for this good. Were production at 15 thousand pounds, Pareto improvements (could/could not) be achieved by increasing output and Pareto improvements (could/could not) be achieved by decreasing output.

b. At 35 thousand pounds, the marginal benefit to some buyer of the last thousand pounds
of shrimp purchased is _____. The marginal cost of producing it at
some firm is _____. Because marginal benefit is (greater than/equal
to/less than) marginal cost, we can deduce that 35 thousand pounds (is/is not) the
economically efficient level of production for this good. Were production at 35 thousand
pounds, Pareto improvements (could/could not) be achieved by increasing output and
Pareto improvements (could/could not) be achieved by decreasing output.

c. At 50 thousand pounds, the marginal benefit to some buyer of the last thousand pounds
of shrimp purchased is _____. The marginal cost of producing it at
some firm is _____. Because marginal benefit is (greater than/equal
to/less than) marginal cost, we can deduce that 50 thousand pounds (is/is not) the
economically efficient level of production for this good. Were production at 50 thousand
pounds, Pareto improvements (could/could not) be achieved by increasing output and
Pareto improvements (could/could not) be achieved by decreasing output.

2. Gillette's trademark gives it a monopoly in the market for Atra^{TM} razor blades. Suppose that
weekly market demand for 10-packs of Atra^{TM} blades in the Southwestern market area is
known to be

$$P = 10 - 0.25Q,$$

where Q is thousands of packs per week. Gillete's marginal revenue from sales in this
market area will therefore be

$$MR = 10 - 0.5Q.$$

Suppose that Gillette's marginal cost of producing these blades increases with output, and is
given by

$$MC = 1 + 0.25Q.$$

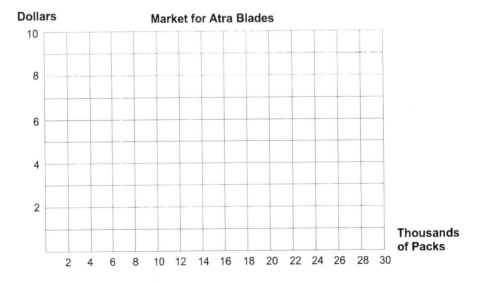

a. Plot Gillette's demand curve, marginal revenue curve, and marginal cost curve on the grid provided.

b. To maximize profit, Gillette should produce where (demand equals supply/marginal revenue equals marginal cost/demand equals marginal cost). The level of output that maximizes profit is _____ thousand packs per week. Gillette will sell this output at a price of _____ dollars per pack.

c. At Gillette's profit-maximizing output, the marginal benefit of the last pack produced to some buyer in the market is _____ dollars. The marginal cost to Gillette of that last pack produced is _____ dollars. From this we can deduce that Gillette (does/does not) produce the economically efficient level of output for this market.

d. If the government wanted to compel Gillette to produce the economically efficient level of output in this market, how much output should it compel Gillette to produce? _____ At this level of output, the marginal benefit to some buyer of the last pack consumed is (greater than/equal to/less than) the marginal cost to Gillette of the last pack produced.

3. The metropolitan market for bicycles is perfectly competitive. Monthly market demand and market supply are

$$Q^D = 225 - P$$
$$Q^S = P - 25$$

where P is price, Q^D is quantity demanded, and Q^S is quantity supplied.

a. Plot the market demand and market supply curves.

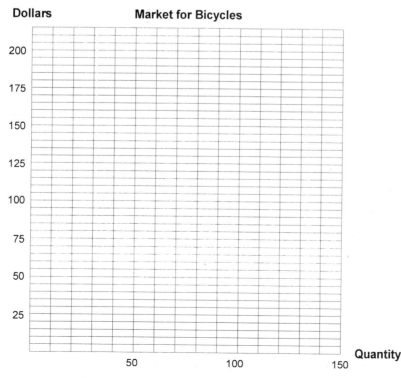

b. What is the equilibrium price in this market? _____ What is the equilibrium quantity? _____

c. The city council thinks that bikes are just too expensive in their town, so they've decided to implement a set of price controls: From now on, the price of bikes can be no higher than $105. Draw a horizontal line on your diagram to indicate the maximum legal price per bike.

d. As a result of these controls, buyers will buy (fewer/more) bikes and pay a (higher/lower) price per bike: sellers will sell (fewer/more) bikes and receive a (higher/lower) price per bike. Under these price controls, the market price per bike will be _____ dollars, and a total of _____ bikes will be bought and sold.

e. At the market equilibrium you just found in (d), the marginal benefit to some consumer of consuming an additional bicycle is _____. The marginal cost to some firm of producing that additional bicycle is _____. Because the marginal benefit of an additional bicycle is (greater than/equal to/less than) its marginal cost, the market equilibrium under these price controls (is/is not) efficient.

15-MINUTE PRACTICE TEST

Set a timer, giving yourself just 15 minutes to answer all of the following questions. To see what you *really* know and remember, take the test at least a day *after* you've read the chapter in the text and completed the exercises in this study guide.

Multiple Choice: Circle the letter in front of the single best answer.

1. A Pareto improvement is best defined as any change in which
   a. at least one person gains and no one is harmed.
   b. many people gain and no one is harmed.
   c. the gains to the gainers are greater than the losses to the losers.
   d. the gainers are forced to compensate the losers for their losses.
   e. the losers are forced to compensate the gainers to prevent the change.

2. Some actions which by themselves are not Pareto improvements can be *converted* into Pareto improvements by using
   a. an imperfectly competitive market.
   b. a mixture of labor and capital.
   c. fewer resources.
   d. a side payment.
   e. a price ceiling.

3. In a productively inefficient economy, it is possible to produce more of some good
    a. only by using more resources.
    b. only by producing less of some other good.
    c. only by producing more of some other good.
    d. without producing less of any other good.
    e. by changing from perfectly to imperfectly competitive markets.

4. As a rule, when a market is imperfectly competitive, economic efficiency is not achieved because the price is
    a. too high, and too little of the good is produced.
    b. too low, and too little of the good is produced.
    c. too low, and too much of the good is produced.
    d. too high, and too much of the good is produced.
    e. right and the amount produced is right, but the wrong consumers end up with the good.

5. Which of the following would *not* be a Pareto improvement?
    a. You pay $9 for a movie ticket and enjoy the movie.
    b. The economy stops producing a good that no one wants, and uses the freed-up inputs to produce a good that some people want.
    c. The government eliminates all regulations on food safety, and production of food rises dramatically.
    d. A collector of comic books buys a rare comic for $2,000.
    e. None of the above (i.e., all of the above are Pareto improvements)

6. If the marginal product of pretzel machines in firm A is 8, and the marginal product of pretzel machines in firm B is 6, then
    a. the economy is productively efficient, but not allocatively efficient.
    b. moving pretzel machines from firm A to firm B would increase the output of pretzels.
    c. confiscating a pretzel machine from firm B and giving it to firm A would be a Pareto improvement.
    d. All of the above.
    e. None of the above.

7. Which of the following guarantees that the economy is allocatively efficient?
    a. The economy is productively efficient.
    b. The economy is economically efficient.
    c. There are Pareto improvements that have not yet been exploited.
    d. Markets are imperfectly competitive.
    e. The economy is operating on its PPF.

8. We know that the economy is on its PPF when
    a. markets are imperfectly competitive.
    b. there is full employment of resources.
    c. the economy is productively efficient.
    d. the marginal product of labor is equal to the marginal product of capital at all firms.
    e. none of the above.

9. The height of the market demand curve at any quantity tells us
   a. the marginal cost—to some firm—of the last unit produced.
   b. the average cost—to some firm—of all units produced.
   c. the marginal benefit—to some consumer—of the last unit consumed.
   d. the average benefit—to all consumers—of all units consumed.
   e. the marginal product of labor at some firm.

10. One reason that imperfectly competitive markets do not take advantage of many Pareto improvements is that
    a. they are not trying to maximize profits.
    b. they are not trying to minimize costs.
    c. the cannot price discriminate.
    d. they do not use all of the resources at their disposal.
    e. they do not pay their resources as much as other firms would.

True/False: For each of the following statements, circle T if the statement is true or F if the statement is false.

T   F   1. Economic efficiency requires that all Pareto improvements be exploited.

T   F   2. If a change occurs in which some people lose, but a side payment more-than-compensates the losers, then the final result is a Pareto improvement.

T   F   3. Any change that is a Pareto improvement will tend to make the economy more fair.

T   F   4. If you are desperately hungry, and you buy a loaf of bread from the only food store in town for $500, then you have been exploited so the purchase is *not* a Pareto improvement.

T   F   5. Any economy which is productively efficient is also allocatively efficient.

T   F   6. If we find two firms that produce the same output, and the marginal product of labor is different in these firms, then we know that the industry in question is productively inefficient.

T   F   7. Full employment of resources guarantees allocative efficiency.

T   F   8. The economy of the former Soviet Union was productively efficient, but not allocatively efficient.

CHAPTER 15

GOVERNMENT'S ROLE IN ECONOMIC EFFICIENCY

Fill in each blank with the appropriate word or phrase from the list provided in the word bank. (For a challenge, fill in as many blanks as you can *without* using the word bank.)

_____ 1. A wrongful act that harms someone.

_____ 2. A market equilibrium that fails to take advantage of every Pareto improvement.

_____ 3. The regulatory strategy of setting price equal to a natural monopoly's long run average total cost.

_____ 4. The tendency of regulated natural monopolies to overinvest in capital.

_____ 5. A by-product of a good or activity that affects someone not immediately involved in the transaction.

_____ 6. A good that is nonrival and nonexcludable.

_____ 7. A good that is rival and excludable.

_____ 8. A situation in which one person's consumption of a good or service means than no one else can consume it.

_____ 9. The ability to prevent those who do not pay for a good from consuming it.

_____ 10. The problem of overuse when a good is rivalrous but nonexcludable.

_____ 11. The sum of squared market shares of all firms in an industry.

Word Bank

average cost pricing
Averich-Johnson effect
excludability
externality
Herfindahl-Hirschman Index
market failure

private good
public good
rivalry
tort
tragedy of the commons

CHAPTER HIGHLIGHTS

Fill in the blanks with the appropriate words or phrases. If you have difficulty, review the chapter and then try again.

1. By making most involuntary exchanges illegal, _____ law channels our energies into activities that increase economic efficiency.

2. Countries with poorly defined _____ rights do not produce as much output from their resources as they could with better-defined _____ rights. Greater output could make some people better off without harming anyone—a _____ improvement. Thus, countries with poorly defined _____ rights are economically _____.

3. _____ enable us to make exchanges that take place over time and in which one person must act first. In this way, _____ help society enjoy the full benefits of specialization and _____.

4. A legal and _____ system that ensured the complete elimination of crime, unsafe products, and other unwelcome activities would be less _____ than a system that tolerated some amount of these activities.

5. Taxes can make a market more or less _____, depending on the nature of the tax and the initial conditions of the market.

6. Raising general tax revenue with excise taxes is inefficient, since it creates a situation in which the _____ for a consumer is greater than the _____ to some producer. Hence, too _____ of the taxed goods will be produced and consumed.

7. When a government service is used along with a market good, it is efficient for the government to charge a (an) _____ tax on the good equal to the _____ of providing the government service used with that good.

8. Since the government can't function without taxes, and the only efficient taxes are unfair, we tolerate the _____ that taxes cause.

9. With average cost pricing for a natural monopoly, regulators strive to set the price equal to cost per unit where the _____ curve crosses the _____ curve. At this price, the natural monopoly makes _____ economic profit, which provides its owners with a fair rate of return and keeps the monopoly in business.

10. An externality is a _____ of a good or activity that affects someone not immediately involved in the transaction

11. A market with a negative externality associated with producing or consuming a good will be inefficient. In market equilibrium, the _____ to all parties will exceed the _____ to all parties.

12. A tax equal to the difference between marginal _____ and marginal _____ can correct a negative externality and make a market efficient.

13. A market with a positive externality associated with producing or consuming a good will be inefficient. In market equilibrium, the _____ to all parties will exceed the _____ of the good.

14. A subsidy equal to the difference between marginal _____ and marginal _____ can correct a positive externality and make a market efficient.

15. If there is rivalry in consumption of a good, the _____ should provide it.

16. Private goods have two characteristics: _____ and _____.
    Because of _____, the market *should* provide the good, and because of _____, the market *will* provide the good.

17. When a good is nonexcludable, people have an incentive to become _____—to let others pay for the good, so they can enjoy it without paying.

18. When a good is nonexcludable, the _____ will not provide it. If we want such a good, _____ must provide it.

19. When a good or service is nonrival, the market cannot provide it efficiently. Rather, to achieve economic efficiency, the good or service would have to be provided at a price equal to _____.

20. _____ can make a market more competitive, with lower prices, by breaking a monopolist into several competing companies. It can also sustain competition by preventing _____ between large competitors.

21. In practice, _____ often has the undesirable effect of preventing the entry of new competitors into the market. When that occurs, the removal of _____ will result in increased competition and lower prices.

IMPORTANT CONCEPTS

Write a brief answer below each of the following questions.

1. List the five types of law that contribute to economic efficiency.

   a. _____ law   d. _____ law

   b. _____ law   e. _____ law

   c. _____ law

2. Indicate whether this statement is true or false, and explain briefly: "While raising general tax revenue with an excise tax is inefficient, doing so with an income tax is entirely efficient."

3. List three different types of market failures

   a.

   b.

   c.

4. In the blanks below, state the specific type of market failure represented by each of the following situations:

   a. A noisy dance club opens in your neighborhood, causing noise and traffic at all hours of the night. _____

   b. All of the gas stations in your town except one go out of business. The remaining gas station raises its prices. _____

   c. Your neighbors shovel the snow off of the sidewalk in front of their houses, making it easier for you, as well as them, to walk to the bus stop. _____

   d. Everyone in a city would benefit if more trees were planted along sidewalks, but no firm will plant them because it would be impossible to charge those who benefit by walking by_____.

5. In the blanks below, list the two characteristics of a pure private good, and the two characteristics of a pure public good.

   a. Pure private good: _____ and _____

   b. Pure public good: _____ and _____

SKILLS AND TOOLS

For the following items, follow the instructions, write the correct answer in the blanks, or circle the correct answer.

1. Remember our analysis of the metropolitan market for bicycles in the previous chapter? Monthly market demand and market supply in that perfectly competitive market are

$$Q^D = 225 - P$$
$$Q^S = P - 25$$

where P is price, Q^D is quantity demanded, and Q^S is quantity supplied.

a. Plot the market demand and market supply curves.

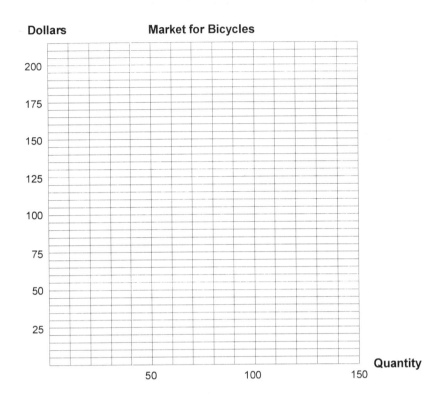

Dollars   **Market for Bicycles**

200

175

150

125

100

75

50

25

                    50   100   150   **Quantity**

b. What is the equilibrium price in this market? _____ What is the equilibrium
    quantity? _____

c. Suppose the City Council now decides to raise some revenue by imposing a $40 excise
    tax on each bicycle sold. Draw the resulting market supply when firms must pay this
    excise tax.

d. In the new equilibrium, what price (inclusive of tax) do consumers pay? _____
    What price (after paying the tax) do producers receive? _____ What is the
    new equilibrium quantity? _____

e. As a result of this tax, the price that consumers pay for a bicycle has (risen/fallen) by
    _____ dollars. The price that producers receive for a bicycle has (risen/
    fallen) by _____ dollars. After this tax is imposed, the difference between
    the price consumers pay and the price producers receive is_____ dollars, an
    amount (larger than/just equal to/less than) the excise tax imposed.

f. At the after-tax market equilibrium you just found in (d), the marginal benefit to some
    consumer of consuming an additional bicycle is _____ . The marginal cost
    to some firm of producing that additional bicycle is _____. Because the

marginal benefit of an additional bicycle is (greater than/equal to/less than) its marginal cost, the market equilibrium after the excise tax is imposed (is/is not) efficient.

2. Cell-U was first to perfect low-power campus-wide wireless communication for university students. Using their own technology and a single centrally-located antenna on campus, the company can provide student customers with a convenient bare-bones service which the company calls, ``Cell-U-*Lite.*''

The company's *LRATC* curve is drawn on the grid below, where Q is thousands of calls per week. It has found that the marginal cost of an additional phone call over its campus network is always constant and equal to 10 cents, so for this firm MC=10.

Demand for this service on one university campus is given by

$$P = 40 - (1/8)Q,$$

where P is cents and Q is thousands of calls per week. Cell-U's marginal revenue is therefore

$$MR = 40 - (1/4)Q.$$

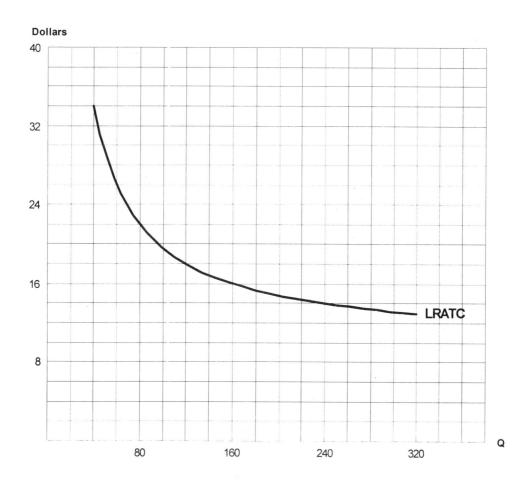

a. Because its *LRATC* curve is everywhere downward sloping, Cell-U will be a (natural disaster/natural competitor/natural monopoly) on campus.

b. Plot Cell-U's demand and marginal revenue curves on the grid provided. Plots its marginal cost curve too.

c. If Cell-U is allowed to choose output to maximize its own profit, it will service _____ thousand calls per week, and it will charge _____ cents per call. From the graph, we can see that the long run average total cost of that many calls is _____ cents per call. Cell-U's weekly profit from this campus-wide market will therefore be _____ dollars per week.

d. The level of output that maximizes this firm's profit (is/is not) economically efficient because if an additional unit were produced and sold, it would have a value to some consumer of _____ cents, while the additional cost to produce that additional unit would be _____ cents. The government (can/can not) intervene in this market to increase efficiency.

e. If the government were to require this firm to charge a price equal to marginal cost, how much would Cell-U charge per call? _____ How many calls would it service each month? _____ Under this form of regulation, Cell-U (would/would not) produce and sell the economically efficient level of output, and the firm would (suffer a loss/reap a profit) of approximately _____ dollars each week. Thus, if required to set price equal to marginal cost, Cell-U will provide the economically efficient level of output (no matter what/only if the firm also receives a subsidy to cover its losses/and generate tax revenue for the government as well).

f. If, instead, the government were to regulate Cell-U's price so that the firm was able to earn no more than a fair rate of return, Cell-U would choose to service (approximately) _____ thousand calls per week. The firm would charge a price of (approximately) _____ cents per call, and earn a profit of _____ dollars per week under this form of regulation. The level of output Cell-U would produce under this form of regulation is therefore (higher than/equal to/lower than) the monopoly level of output and (higher than/equal to/lower than) the economically efficient level of output.

g. Under rate of return regulation, this firm will still charge a price that is (greater than/equal to/ less than) marginal cost, and so produce a level of output that is (greater than/equal to/less than) the economically efficient level in this market. However, the difference between price charged and marginal cost of additional output under rate of return regulation is (lower than/equal to /greater than) the difference between price and marginal cost when the firm is completely unregulated.

3. In Manila, capital of the Philippines, a favorite form of transportation is the colorful "Jeepney," an elaborately decorated US Army surplus Jeep modified to carry passengers for hire. Because there are so many of them in the city, Jeepney traffic is a major contributor to Manila's air pollution problem.

   Suppose it has been determined that the marginal social cost of Jeepney rides in Metro-Manila is given by the equation

$$MSC = 1 + 0.01Q$$

where Q is the quantity of rides per day. In addition, the daily market demand and market supply of Jeepney rides in the purely competitive Metro-Manila market are plotted below.

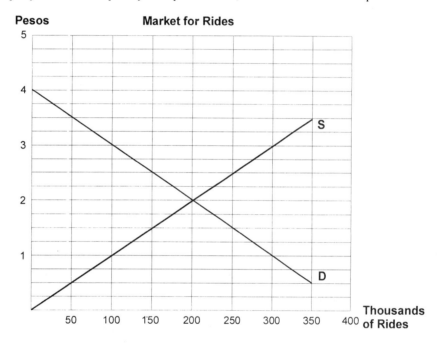

a. Plot the marginal social cost (MSC) curve on the grid provided.

b. In the absence of government involvement, the equilibrium price of a Jeepney ride will be _____ peso(s). The equilibrium quantity of Jeepney rides will be _____ thousand per day.

c. The competitive equilibrium in this market (is/is not) efficient: the equilibrium quantity of Jeepney rides produced and consumed is (too high/just right/too low). This is clear because, in equilibrium, the marginal benefit derived from the last ride consumed is (greater than/equals to/less than) the marginal social cost of producing it.

d. To ensure that the efficient quantity of rides is produced and consumed each day, the government should (levy a tax of 1 peso per ride on Jeepneys/provide a subsidy of 1 peso per ride to Jeepneys). This will (raise/lower) the marginal private cost of a Jeepney ride and cause the market (demand/supply) curve to shift (rightward/leftward). The equilibrium price of rides produced will (increase/decrease) to _____ peso(s), and the quantity of rides produced and consumed will (increase/decrease) to _____ thousand rides per day.

e. The new equilibrium achieved after imposition of the 1 peso tax (will/will not) be efficient. In this new equilibrium, the marginal benefit derived from the last ride consumed is (greater than/equal to/less than) the marginal social cost of producing it.

4. Industries A, B, and C each have five firms. The firms' market shares in these three industries are reported in the table.

	Industry A	Industry B	Industry C
Firm 1	40%	60%	25%
Firm 2	30%	10%	25%
Firm 3	20%	10%	25%
Firm 4	5%	10%	25%
Firm 5	5%	10%	0%

a. Calculate the Herfindahl-Hirschman Index for each industry:

The HHI in Industry A is _____.

The HHI in Industry B is _____.

The HHI in Industry C is _____.

b. According to the HHI, which market is the most concentrated? _____

5. Suppose there are six firms in the market for facial beauty soap. Data on the market share of each producer is given in the table.

Producer	Market Share
Golden Glow	10%
Peachy Clean	10%
Avocado Smooth	20%
Silky Clean	20%
Perfect Skin	25%
Ebony Satin	15%

a. What is the Herfindahl-Hirschman Index for this industry? _____

b. Ebony Satin and Avocado Smooth have proposed to merge. If they merge, what will be the Herfindhal-Hirschman Index for this industry? _____ Thus, the proposed merger would (increase/decrease) the HHI in this industry by _____ points.

c. According to its current guidelines, the Justice Department (would/would not) consider challenging the proposed merger between Ebony Satin and Avocado Smooth.

15-MINUTE PRACTICE TEST

Set a timer, giving yourself just 15 minutes to answer all of the following questions. To see what you *really* know and remember, take the test at least a day *after* you've read the chapter in the text and completed the exercises in this study guide.

Multiple Choice: Circle the letter in front of the single best answer.

1. Which type of law sets up incentives against injuries that result from accidents and other events?
   a. Criminal law
   b. Property law
   c. Contract law
   d. Tort law
   e. Antitrust law

2. Which of the following activities is restricted in some way by U.S. antitrust law?
   a. Agreements among competitors
   b. Mergers
   c. Formation of a monopoly
   d. All of the above
   e. None of the above

3. If an excise tax were imposed on good X, then
   a. the price of good X to consumers will increase.
   b. the marginal cost to some producer will be greater than the marginal benefit to some consumer.
   c. the demand curve for good X will shift rightward.
   d. all of the above.
   e. none of the above.

4. An excise tax on a good is efficient when
   a. the good is beneficial to society.
   b. the good is a pure private good.
   c. the good is a pure public good.
   d. the good is provided in an imperfectly competitive market.
   e. a government service is provided along with the good.

5. Which of the following is *not* an example of a market failure?

    a. A imperfectly competitive market
    b. A positive externality
    c. A negative externality
    d. A good characterized by nonrivalry and nonexcludability
    e. A good that few people want

6. An efficient way to correct a *negative* externality is to impose a _____ equal to the difference between the _____ and the _____ of providing the good.

    a. subsidy; marginal private cost; marginal private benefit
    b. subsidy; marginal private cost; marginal social benefit
    c. tax; marginal social cost; marginal private cost
    d. tax; marginal private cost; marginal private benefit
    e. tax or subsidy; marginal cost; average cost

7. An efficient way to correct a *positive* externality is to impose a _____ equal to the difference between the _____ and the _____ of providing the good.

    a. subsidy; marginal social benefit; marginal private benefit
    b. subsidy; marginal private cost; marginal social benefit
    c. tax; marginal social cost; marginal private cost
    d. tax; marginal private cost; marginal social benefit
    e. tax or subsidy; marginal cost; average cost

8. A pure public good is characterized by

    a. excludability and rivalry.
    b. excludability and nonrivalry.
    c. nonexcludability and rivalry.
    d. nonexcludability and nonrivalry.
    e. excludability, rivalry, and a negative or positive externality.

9. The "free rider" problem is defined as the problem that arises when

    a. a public transport worker cannot properly check for tickets because he is distracted by traffic or other conditions.
    b. fleas or other parasites travel from person to person undetected.
    c. a good is nonexcludable.
    d. a good is nonrival.
    e. a good is a pure private good.

10. Which of the following is an illustration of the "tragedy of the commons"?

    a. Too few people go to college because it is so expensive.
    b. The government makes weather reports available free of charge.
    c. Netscape goes out of business, leaving Microsoft as the only Internet browser available to PC users.
    d. A high quality television program is taken off the air because too few people watch it.
    e. City streets are overcrowded at rush hour.

True/False: For each of the following statements, circle T if the statement is true or F if the statement is false.

T   F   1. Surprisingly, the data show only a weak or non-existent correlation between the quality of the institutional infrastructure and output per worker.

T   F   2. An important economic contribution made by criminal law is to limit transactions to those that benefit both sides.

T   F   3. While legal procedures tell businesses what to do, regulation typically imposes fines or other penalties if businesses do something wrong.

T   F   4. The existence of even small amounts of crime, unsafe products and other activities that harm society is evidence of economic inefficiency.

T   F   5. Raising general tax revenue with an excise tax is inefficient because it reduces output of the taxed good, and creates a situation in which the marginal benefit to a consumer exceeds the marginal cost to some producer.

T   F   6. A tax on wages is efficient because it moves the labor market from one efficient equilibrium to another efficient equilibrium.

T   F   7. While negative externalities represent a market failure, positive externalities do not.

T   F   8. Urban parks are characterized by both nonrivalry and nonexcludability.

CHAPTER 16

COMPARATIVE ADVANTAGE
AND THE GAINS FROM TRADE

SPEAKING ECONOMICS

Fill in each blank with the appropriate word or phrase from the list provided in the word bank. (For a challenge, fill in as many blanks as you can *without* using the word bank.)

_____ 1. Goods and services produced domestically, but sold abroad.

_____ 2. Goods and services produced abroad, but consumed domestically.

_____ 3. The ability to produce a good using fewer resources than another country.

_____ 4. The ability to produce a good at a lower opportunity cost than elsewhere.

_____ 5. The ratio at which a country can trade domestically produced products for foreign-produced products.

_____ 6. The amount of one currency that is traded for one unit of another currency.

_____ 7. A tax on imports.

_____ 8. A limit on the physical volume of imports.

_____ 9. A belief that a nation should keep foreign goods out of domestic markets to benefit domestic industries.

Word Bank

absolute advantage
comparative advantage
exchange rate
exports
imports

protectionism
quota
tariff
terms of trade

CHAPTER HIGHLIGHTS

Fill in the blanks with the appropriate words or phrases. If you have difficulty, review the chapter and then try again.

1. A nation has an absolute advantage in producing a good if it can produce it _____ than another country, and a comparative advantage if it can produce the good _____ than another country.

2. If countries specialize according to _____, a more efficient use of given resources occurs. As a result, the world can produce more of at least one good, without producing _____ of any other good.

3. As long as _____ differ, specialization and trade can be beneficial to all involved. This remains true regardless of whether the parties involved are nations, states, counties, or individuals. It remains true even if one party holds an all-round _____ advantage or disadvantage.

4. When consumers are free to buy at the lowest prices, they will naturally buy a good from the country that has a comparative advantage in producing it. A country's industries respond by producing more of that good and less of other goods. In this way, countries naturally tend to _____ in those goods in which they have a comparative advantage.

5. Countries often specialize in products based on their own particular endowments of _____. But _____ are not the only bases for comparative advantage.

6. Countries often develop strong _____ in the goods they have produced in the _____, regardless of why they began producing those goods in the first place.

7. When the opening of trade results in increased exports of a good, the _____ of the good are made better off and will support increased trade. _____ of the good will be made worse off and will oppose increased trade.

8. When the opening of trade results in increased imports of a product, the domestic _____ of the product are made worse off and will oppose the increased trade. _____ are better off and will favor increased trade.

9. Tariffs _____ the volume of trade and _____ the domestic prices of imported goods. In the country that imposes the tariff,

_____ gain and _____ lose. But the world as a whole _____, because tariffs _____ the volume of trade and therefore _____ the gains from trade.

10. Quotas have effects similar to tariffs—they _____ the quantity of imports and _____ domestic prices. While both measures help domestic producers, they _____ the benefits of trade to the nation as a whole. However, a tariff has one saving grace: _____.

11. Production is most likely to reflect the principle of _____ when firms can obtain funds for investment projects and when they can freely enter industries that are profitable. Thus, free trade, without government intervention, works best when markets are working well.

IMPORTANT CONCEPTS

Write a brief answer below each of the following questions.

1. What is the key difference between the principles of *absolute* advantage and *comparative* advantage? Which of the two determines the goods and services a country will produce and export?

2. List three reasons why nations might *not* trade according to their comparative advantage, or not completely specialize when they trade with other nations. (Your text discusses four reasons.)

   a.

   b.

   c.

3. Suppose that when trade opens up between two countries, Country A exports good X and Country B exports good Y. In the table below, state how each group is affected by filling in each cell with the word "gain" or "lose." For example, in the leftmost, top cell, state whether producers of good X in Country A gain or lose when trade opens up.

	Country A		Country B	
	Producers of:	Consumers of:	Producers of:	Consumers of:
Good X				
Good Y				

4. Do the total gains and total losses cancel each other out? How do you know?

5. Now suppose that Country A and Country B have been trading for years, and one day Country A decides to impose a tariff on imports of Good Y from Country B. In the table below, state how each group is affected by filling in each cell with the word "gain" or "lose."

	Country A		Country B	
	Producers of:	Consumers of:	Producers of:	Consumers of:
Good Y				

6. What is the "infant industry argument?" Is it an argument in favor of, or against, protectionism?

7. Indicate whether this statement is true or false, and explain briefly: "When a high-wage country trades with a low-wage country, the high-wage country's goods cannot compete, and the high-wage country's residents are made worse off by trade."

SKILLS AND TOOLS

For the following items, follow the instructions, write the correct answer in the blank, or circle the correct answer.

1. Data on the costs of producing bicycles and VCRs in Germany and the US are provided in the table. Assume all resources in each country are (and remain) fully employed. Assume costs, expressed in the relevant currency, remain constant no matter how much is produced.

<table>
<tr><td></td><td colspan="2" align="center">**Costs of Production**</td></tr>
<tr><td></td><td align="center">**Per Bicycle**</td><td align="center">**Per VCR**</td></tr>
<tr><td>**Germany**</td><td align="center">DM200</td><td align="center">DM400</td></tr>
<tr><td>**United States**</td><td align="center">$300</td><td align="center">$900</td></tr>
</table>

a. Suppose Germany produced one additional VCR. This would require Germany to divert resources worth DM_____ from bicycle production. Since each bike uses up resources worth DM_____, producing one additional VCR requires that Germany produce _____ fewer (bicycles/VCRs). In Germany, the opportunity cost of an additional VCR is therefore _____ (bicycles/VCRs).

b. Suppose the United States produced one additional VCR. This would require the United States to divert resources worth _____ from bicycle production. Since each bicycle uses up resources worth _____, producing one additional VCR requires that the United States produce _____ fewer (bicycles/VCRs). In the United States, the opportunity cost of an additional VCR is therefore _____ (bicycles/VCRs).

c. Carry forward your answers to (a) and (b), then compute the remaining opportunity costs to complete the table.

<table>
<tr><td></td><td colspan="2" align="center">**Opportunity Costs**</td></tr>
<tr><td></td><td align="center">**Per Bicycle**</td><td align="center">**Per VCR**</td></tr>
<tr><td>**Germany**</td><td align="center">_____</td><td align="center">_____</td></tr>
<tr><td>**United States**</td><td align="center">_____</td><td align="center">_____</td></tr>
</table>

d. From this table, we can see that Germany has a comparative advantage in producing _____ while the United States has a comparative advantage in producing _____. This is because the opportunity cost of _____ in Germany is less than it is in the United States, while the opportunity cost of _____ in the United States is less than it is in Germany.

2. Let's continue with the data from the previous question and consider the gains from specialization and exchange.

   a. To achieve gains from trade, Germany should produce more _____ and fewer _____, while the United States should produce more _____ and fewer _____. Germany should then export _____ to the United States and import _____ from the United States, while the United States should export _____ to Germany and import _____ from Germany.

   b. As an example of the potential for gain through specialization and trade, suppose that Germany diverts enough resources from bicycles to produce an additional 25 VCRs, while the United States diverts enough resources from VCRs to produce an additional 60 bicycles. Complete the table.

   | | **A Change in Production** | |
	Bicycle Production	**VCR Production**
Germany	_____	+25
United States	+60	_____
World	_____	_____

   c. To show that both sides can gain from trade, let us suppose that production in each country has shifted as in (b). Suppose that trade is opened between the two countries and that:

   Germany exports (and the U.S. imports) 22 VCRs

   Germany imports (and the U.S. exports) 55 bicycles.

   Complete the following table.

   | | **The Gains from Specialization and Trade** | | |
	Production	**Loss from exports (–) or gain from imports (+)**	**Net Gain**
Germany			
Bicycles	–50	+55	_____
VCRs	_____	–22	_____
United States			
Bicycles	60	–55	_____
VCRs	_____	+22	_____

d. In the example of part (c), the United States exports 55 bicycles in exchange for 22 VCRs. The **terms of trade** in this example are therefore _____ bicycles for 1 VCR. At these terms of trade, our example has shown that (only Germany/only the United States/both Germany and the United States) can gain from specialization and trade. This is clear from the table in part (c): the gains from trade for the United States are _____ bicycles and _____ VCRs, while the gains from trade for Germany are _____ bicycles and _____ VCRs.

3. The French and Israelis both consume oranges. France and Israel are also both capable of producing oranges. Domestic demand and domestic supply of oranges in each country are provided below.

For simplicity, P is the price per pound of oranges *measured in U.S. dollars*, and Q is thousands of kilos per month.

	Domestic Demand	**Domestic Supply**
France	$Q^D = \dfrac{4400}{6} - \dfrac{400P}{3}$	$Q^S = \dfrac{200P}{3} - \dfrac{200}{3}$
Israel	$Q^D = \dfrac{1100}{3} - \dfrac{200P}{3}$	$Q^S = \dfrac{500}{3} + \dfrac{400P}{3}$

a. Plot these demand and supply curves in the grids provided.

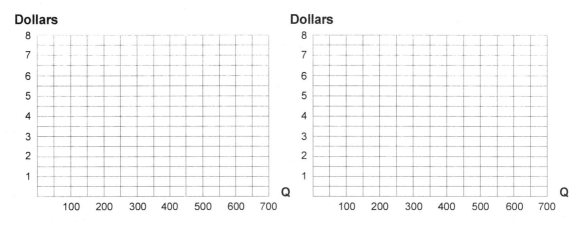

b. If France and Israel do not trade with one another, the price of oranges in France will be _____ dollars and the quantity of oranges produced and consumed will be _____ thousand kilos per month. In Israel, the price of oranges will be _____ dollars and the quantity of oranges produced and consumed will be _____ thousand kilos per month.

c. If free trade in oranges is opened between these two countries, France will (import/export/neither import nor export) oranges, while Israel will (import/export/neither import nor export) oranges.

d.   With free trade, the price of oranges in France will (rise/fall/remain unchanged) while the price oranges in Israel will (rise/fall/remain unchanged). As this occurs, the quantity of oranges consumed in France will (increase/decrease/remain unchanged), while the quantity of oranges produced in France will (increase/decrease/remain unchanged). In Israel, the price of oranges will (rise/fall/remain unchanged). As this occurs, the quantity of oranges consumed in Israel will (increase/decrease/remain unchanged), while the quantity of oranges produced will (increase/decrease/remain unchanged).

e.   As a result of trade, French consumers pay (higher/lower) prices for oranges, and so will be (better off/worse off) with trade. French orange producers receive (higher/lower) prices for oranges, and so will be (better off/worse off) with trade. At the same time, Israeli consumers pay (higher/lower) prices for oranges, and so will be (better off/worse off) with trade. Israeli orange producers receive (higher/lower) prices for oranges, and so will be (better off/worse off) with trade.

4.   As a challenge, let's determine the exact price of oranges after free trade is opened between France and Israel.

In the text, you learned that after trade is opened, one country's imports must equal the other country's exports in the final market equilibrium. Because imports at any price are the amount by which domestic demand exceeds domestic supply, the equation for French orange imports can be found by subtracting quantity demanded from quantity supplied. Using France's demand and supply equations from question (3), compute the quantity of French orange imports. _____

Similarly, exports at any price will be the amount by which domestic production exceeds domestic consumption. The equation for Israeli orange exports can be found using the Israel's equations in question (3) by subtracting quantity supplied from quantity demanded. Thus, the quantity of Israeli orange exports is _____.

To find the post-trade equilibrium price of oranges, set French imports equal to Israeli exports, and solve for *P*.

We conclude that the post-trade market equilibrium price of oranges will be _____ dollars per kilo. (Sketch this onto your graphs in part (a) of the previous question and verify that French imports equal Israeli exports at this price.)

15-MINUTE PRACTICE TEST

Set a timer, giving yourself just 15 minutes to answer all of the following questions. To see what you *really* know and remember, take the test at least a day *after* you've read the chapter in the text and completed the exercises in this study guide.

Multiple Choice: Circle the letter in front of the single best answer.

1. A nation has a comparative advantage in producing some good if
    a. its workers have a lower wage than the workers in other countries.
    b. it can produce the good with less resources than other countries.
    c. it can produce the good with a lower opportunity cost than other countries.
    d. its technology for producing the good is more advanced than in other countries.
    e. all of the above.

Questions 2–4 refer to the following information: In the United States, it takes 10 hours to produce a ton of corn, and 5 hours to produce a ton of wheat. In Mexico, it takes 15 hours to produce a ton of corn, and 10 hours to produce a ton of wheat.

2. In Mexico, the opportunity cost of a ton of wheat is
    a. 2/3 ton of corn.
    b. 1 ton of corn.
    c. 1.5 tons of corn.
    d. 10 tons of corn.
    e. 15 tons of corn.

3. Based on the information given, which of the following statements is true?
    a. The United States has an absolute advantage in both goods.
    b. The United States has a comparative advantage in producing corn.
    c. Mexico has a comparative advantage in producing wheat.
    d. All of the above.
    e. None of the above.

4. If trade opens up between the U.S. and Mexico, and these are the only two goods traded, then
    a. the United States will export both corn and wheat to Mexico.
    b. Mexico will export both corn and wheat to the United States.
    c. Mexico will export corn and the United States will export wheat.
    d. the United States will export corn and Mexico will export wheat.
    e. neither country will export either good; i.e., there will be no trade between these two countries.

5. The "terms of trade" refers to
   a. bilateral agreements between nations to remove tariffs and quotas.
   b. the harm that trade causes to firms, workers and consumers in certain industries.
   c. promises made to those harmed by trade, in order to weaken their support for protectionism.
   d. the additional transportation and other costs exporters and importers must pay.
   e. the exchange ratio between exported and imported goods.

6. An "infant industry" is
   a. any industry that serves newborns.
   b. any industry begun less than 10 years earlier.
   c. any industry in one country that is younger than the same industry in another country.
   d. an industry in which a country *could* have a comparative advantage once that industry was in place.
   e. an industry in which a firm has an absolute, but not a comparative, advantage.

7. When there are increasing, rather than constant, opportunity costs,
   a. our conclusions about which country has a comparative advantage in which good are reversed.
   b. absolute advantage, rather than comparative advantage, determines which country will produce which good.
   c. there will be no gain from trading between nations.
   d. there will be gains from trade, but complete specialization is less likely.
   e. there will be gains grom trade, but only when countries completely specialize.

8. If trade opens up between Country A and Country B, and Country A exports good X while Country B exports good Y, then
   a. the price of good X to consumers in Country A will fall.
   b. the price of good Y to consumers in Country B will fall.
   c. producers of good Y in Country A will gain.
   d. all of the above.
   e. none of the above.

9. One key difference between a quota and a tariff is that
   a. tariffs reduce the volume of trade, while quotas do not.
   b. quotas reduce the volume of trade, while tariffs do not.
   c. tariffs generate revenue for the government, while quotas generally do not.
   d. quotas generate revenue for the government, while tariffs generally do not.
   e. quotas benefit domestic producers of the protected good, while tariffs do not.

10. The argument for "strategic trade policy" is strongest when
    a. the market is dominated by a few large firms.
    b. the country using the policy is very large.
    c. tariffs are already in place.
    d. quotas are already in place.
    e. the opportunity costs of production for both trading partners are identical.

True/False: For each of the following statements, circle T if the statement is true or F if the statement is false.

T   F   1. If a nation has an absolute advantage in producing some good, it will also have a comparative advantage in producing that good.

T   F   2. When trade opens up between two countries, one country generally gains and the other generally loses.

T   F   3. The United States has a comparative advantage in the production of computer software largely because of its endowments of natural resources.

T   F   4. When trade opens up between two countries, consumers in both countries generally gain while producers in both countries generally lose.

T   F   5. When a country imposes a *tariff* on imports of a good, the price of that good to consumers in the *other* country will generally fall.

T   F   6. When a country imposes a *quota* on imports of a good, the price of that good to consumers in the *other* country will generally fall.

T   F   7. A less-advanced, low-productivity country generally does not gain when it trades with a more-advanced, high-productivity country.

T   F   8. The United States is a "free trade" country: it allows foreign goods to be sold in U.S. markets with virtually no restrictions.

ANSWERS TO QUESTIONS

ANSWERS FOR CHAPTER 1

Speaking Economics

1. economics
2. scarcity
3. resources
4. labor
5. capital
6. human capital
7. land
8. microeconomics
9. macroeconomics
10. positive economics
11. normative economics
12. model
13. simplifying assumption
14. critical assumption

Chapter Highlights

1. scarcity
2. resources
3. land; labor; capital
4. micro
5. macro
6. positive
7. normative
8. abstract
9. conclusions
10. critical

Important Concepts

1. a. microeconomic; positive
   b. macroeconomic; positive
   c. microeconomic; positive
   d. microeconomic; normative
   e. macroeconomic; positive
   f. microeconomic; normative
   g. macroeconomic; normative

2. a. labor
   b. capital
   c. capital
   d. land
   e. labor
   f. capital
   g. labor
   h. capital

3. False: The right amount of detail depends on the purpose for which the model will be used. In general, a model should have as few details as possible to accomplish its purpose.
4. False: The two types of assumptions are "simplifying assumptions" and "critical assumptions."

Skills and Tools

1. a.

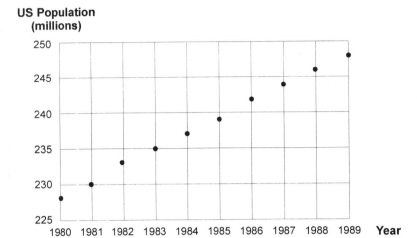

b. (iv)

c.

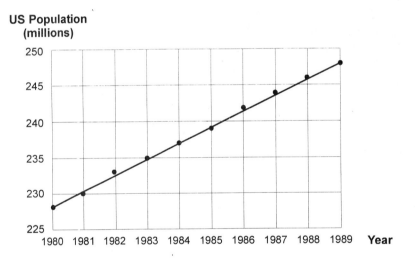

d. Population increased by approximately 2.24 million per year. Your answer can differ from this by a bit because it will depend on how you drew your line with the ruler. To get your answer, though, calculate how much population increased along the vertical axis (the rise) as you move from any one year to the next year along the horizontal axis (the run) on the line you drew.

2. a. 30 to 60; 90 to 120; positive
   b. 0 to 30; 60 to 90; negative
   c. Maximum value of Y = 1,000 is achieved at X = 60; Minimum value of Y = 200 is achieved at X = 90.

3.

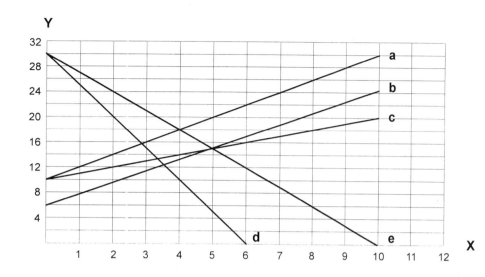

a. 10; 2; increases; constant
b. 5; 2; increases; constant
c. 10; 1; increases; constant
d. 30; –5; decreases; constant
e. 30; –3; decreases; constant

10-Minute Practice Test

Multiple Choice

1. c
2. e
3. d
4. b

4. b
5. c
6. b

True/False

1. F
2. F
3. F

4. T
5. F

ANSWERS FOR CHAPTER 2

Speaking Economics

1. opportunity cost
2. production possibilities frontier (PPF)
3. law of increasing opportunity cost.
4. productive inefficiency
5. specialization
6. exchange
7. absolute advantage
8. comparative advantage
9. resource allocation
10. traditional economy
11. command economy; centrally planned economy
12. market economy
13. market

14. price
15. communism
16. socialism

17. capitalism
18. economic system

Chapter Highlights

1. opportunity cost
2. opportunity cost; resources
3. increasing; greater
4. inefficient
5. specialization; exchange; specialization; exchange

6. absolute advantage
7. comparative advantage
8. comparative advantage
9. command
10. market

Important Concepts

1. False; if the individual had not gone to college, he/she would only have had *one* of the full-time jobs, not all three of them. To determine the foregone income, we would use the job that *would* have been chosen if the person did not go to college. If, for example, the person would have chosen to be a truck driver, then the opportunity cost of a year in college would be the direct money cost of college plus $45,000 in foregone income.

2. The law of increasing opportunity cost.

3. In any order
   (a) productive inefficiency
   (b) recession.

4. In any order
   (a) The development of expertise from specializing in a single task
   (b) the reduction in unproductive time to switch among different tasks
   (c) gains from comparative advantage.

5. Yes, this is consistent with comparative advantage. College professors have a comparative advantage in other activities, such as writing research papers and teaching. The opportunity cost of locating library materials is higher for them than for their students.

6. In any order
   (a) tradition
   (b) command
   (c) the market

7. In any order
   (a) communism
   (b) socialism
   (c) capitalism

8. In any order
   a. market capitalism – resource allocation by the market; private resource ownership
   b. centrally planned capitalism – resource allocation by command; private resource ownership
   c. centrally planned socialism – resource allocation by command; state resource ownership
   d. market socialism – resource allocation by the market; state resource ownership

Skills and Tools

1. a. **Oranges**

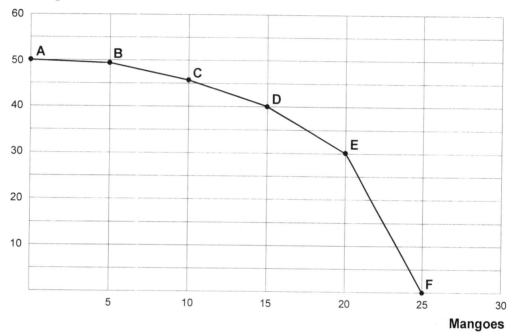

Mangoes

   b. 1; 5; 5; 1
      5; 3; 3
      5; 6; 5; 10; 5; 30
      increasing

   c. 5; 30; 30; 5
      10; 5; 5
      6; 5; 3; 5
      increasing

2. a. are not; zero; zero; no
   b. cannot; improve; acquire more

3. Constant; 50; Y; 50; Y; 50; Y; constant

4. Increases; less than; greater than

5. a. sweaters; fish
   b. 2; 1/3; fish; sweaters

15-Minute Practice Test

Multiple Choice

1. c	6. e
2. d	7. d
3. a	8. c
4. b	9. a
5. b	10. e

True/False

1. F	5. F
2. F	6. T
3. T	7. F
4. T	8. F

ANSWERS FOR CHAPTER 3

Speaking Economics

1. aggregation
2. imperfectly competitive market
3. perfectly competitive market
4. individual's quantity demanded
5. market quantity demanded
6. law of demand
7. demand schedule
8. demand curve
9. change in quantity demanded
10. change in demand
11. income
12. wealth
13. normal good
14. inferior good
15. substitute
16. complement
17. technology
18. firm's quantity supplied
19. market quantity supplied
20. law of supply
21. supply schedule
22. supply curve
23. change in quantity supplied
24. change in supply
25. alternate good
26. equilibrium
27. excess demand
28. excess supply

Chapter Highlights

1. market
2. buyers, sellers (either order)
3. imperfectly competitive
4. competitive (or perfectly competitive); price (or market price)
5. competitive (or perfectly competitive)
6. demanded; price
7. market quantity demanded; price
8. law; fall
9. demand curve; price
10. downward
11. quantity demanded
12. shift; change in demand
13. income, wealth (either order); income, wealth (either order); right
14. increase; right
15. decrease; left
16. technology; inputs; outputs
17. prices; price
18. supplied; price
19. market quantity supplied
20. increase
21. price; price
22. upward
23. quantity supplied
24. shift; change in supply
25. decrease; left
26. rises; falls; left
27. increase; right
28. right
29. decrease; left
30. equilibrium
31. equilibrium; equilibrium
32. left
33. right
34. market; market; market
35. goals; constraints; goals; constraints
36. equilibrium; equilibrium; equilibrium
37. equilibrium

Important Concepts

1. Income (decrease, since it's a normal good); wealth (decrease, since it's a normal good); price of a substitute (decrease); price of a complement (increase); population (decrease); expectations (e.g., an expectation that the price will *fall* in the future); tastes (a change in tastes *away* from the good).

2. Prices of inputs (decrease); profitability of alternate good (decrease); technology (e.g., a cost-saving technological advance); productive capacity (increase, e.g. from an increase in the number of firms); expected future price of the good (decrease).

3. In a perfectly competitive market, there are so many small buyers and sellers that *no one of them can influence the market price*. Each buyer and seller takes the market price as given. In an imperfectly competitive market, at least some buyers or sellers have the ability to influence the price of the product.

4. False. Income is what you earn over a *period* of time. Your wealth is the total value of what you own, minus what you owe, at a given *moment* in time.

5. False. A "change in demand" refers only to a shift in the demand curve. The phrase, "change in quantity demanded" is used for a movement along the demand curve.

Skills and Tools

1. a.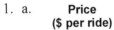

   b. 10; fall; 2; rise; 18

2. a.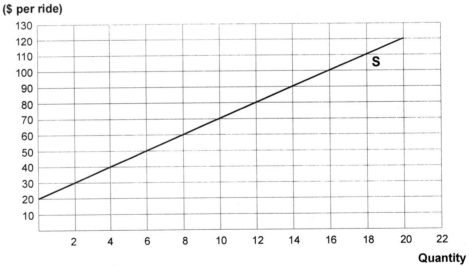

   b. 6; rise; 14; fall; 2

3.

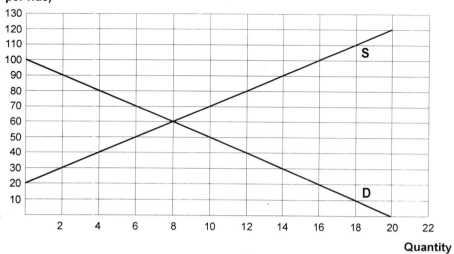

a. 60; 8
b. supply; 8; fall sellers; sell
c. demand; 8; rise; buyers; buy

4. a. $120
b. increase; rightward
c.

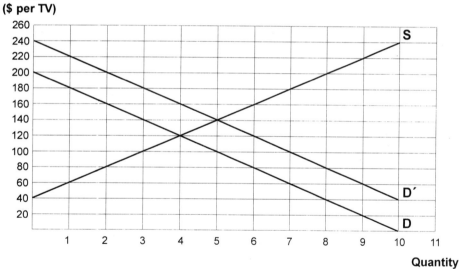

d. Equilibrium price is now $140, where D′ intersects S
e. decrease; leftward

f.

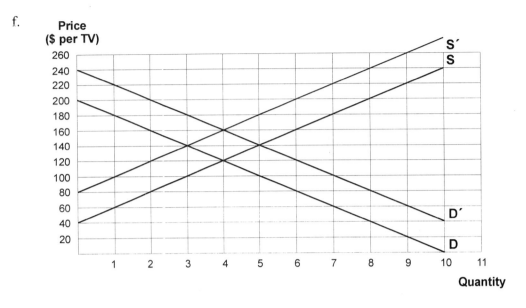

g.   Equilibrium price is now $160, where S′ intersects D′

5. a.

P	Q^D	Q^S
$450	20	80
400	30	70
350	40	60
300	50	50
250	60	40
200	70	30
150	80	20^3

b. supplied; demanded; excess supply; 40; fall; $300
c. demanded; supplied; excess demand; 60; rise; $300

6.

P	Q^D	Q^S
$270	2	20
210	6	15
90	14	5
30	18	0

7. $P_e = \$150$; Yes; 10; Yes

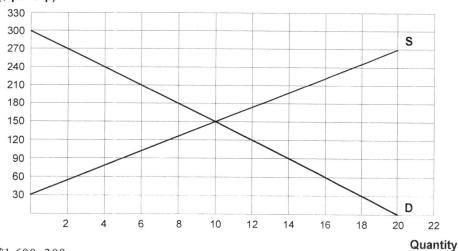

8. a. $1,600; 300

   b. 350; 100; excess demand; 250

   c. 250; 500; excess supply; 250

15-Minute Practice Test

Multiple Choice

1. e	6. b
2. b	7. b
3. d	8. c
4. a	9. b
5. d	10. c

True/False

1. F	5. T
2. F	6. F
3. T	7. F
4. F	8. T

ANSWERS FOR CHAPTER 4

Speaking Economics

1. price ceiling
2. short side of the market
3. black market
4. rent controls
5. price floor
6. excise tax
7. price elasticity of demand
8. inelastic demand
9. perfectly inelastic demand
10. elastic demand
11. perfectly (infinitely) elastic demand
12. unitary elastic
13. short-run elasticity
14. long-run elasticity
15. income elasticity of demand
16. economic necessity
17. economic luxury
18. cross-price elasticity of demand

Chapter Highlights

1. short side
2. ceiling
3. floor; floor; purchasing
4. supply; supply; supply; net
5. rise, fall
6. quantity demanded; price
7. one-
8. elastic
9. inelastic; elastic; unitary elastic
10. expenditure
11. more
12. less
13. long; short; long; short
14. more
15. sellers; buyers
16. quantity demanded; income
17. cross-price

Important Concepts

1. False. A price floor is a minimum price below which the market price is not allowed to fall. If the price floor is set below the equilibrium price, it will have no impact at all on the market, since the equilibrium price is already above the floor.

2. (in any order)
   price elasticity of demand
   income elasticity of demand
   cross-price elasticity of demand

3. (in any order)
   wide availability of substitutes for the good
   the good takes up a relatively large percentage of consumers' budgets

4. a. a positive income elasticity of demand
   b. a negative income elasticity of demand
   c. a positive cross-price elasticity of demand
   d. a negative cross-price elasticity of demand
   e. a negative price elasticity of demand
   f. a price elasticity of demand between 0 and –1.0 (inelastic demand)

5. Neither conclusion is justified. Elasticity is the percentage change in quantity demanded divided by the percentage change in price when a*ll other influences on demand* are held constant. In this city, over the time period specified, other things probably did *not* remain constant. In particular, income, population, the prices of substitutes and complements, and tastes may have changed over the period.

Skills and Tools

1.

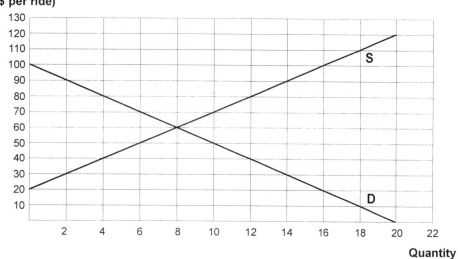

   a. 60; 8
   b. supply; 8
   c. demand; 8
   d. $80

2. a. −2/3
    b. −3/4
    c. −1.852
    d. −1/2
    e. −7/5

3. Same as (a) and (e) above.

4. a.

b. 0; 12; −6; elastic; increase
c. −4/3; elastic; increase
d. −2/5; inelastic; decrease

5 a.

P	Q^D'
1,400	10
1,000	22
600	34
200	46
0	52

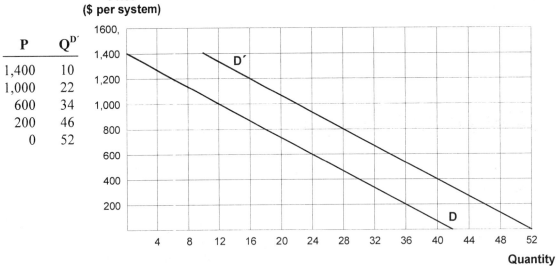

b. −9/4; decreased; −6/7; decreased; −3/10; decreased; decreased

6. a. −2; steeper; −5; 20; 40
   b. 10; 30; −1
   c. 16; 24; −2/5
   d. inelastic

7. a. 1/2
   b. 19/7
   c. 3/2

8. a. -1/2
   b. 0.847

9. a. 1/2
   b. 3/2
   c. 3/4
   d. 0

15-Minute Practice Test

Multiple Choice

1. b
2. d
3. c
4. e
5. b

6. e
7. d
8. b
9. d
10. b

True/False

1. T
2. F
3. T
4. T

5. T
6. F
7. T
8. F

ANSWERS FOR CHAPTER 5

Speaking Economics

1. budget constraint
2. budget line
3. relative price
4. utility
5. marginal utility
6. law of diminishing marginal utility
7. rational preferences
8. marginal decision making
9. individual demand curve
10. substitution effect
11. income effect

Chapter Highlights

1. decision makers; maximizing; constraints
2. budget constraint (or budget line)
3. $-P_x/P_y$
4. increase; decrease; slope
5. rotates
6. marginal utility
7. budget line
8. Marginal Decision Making; marginal
9. per dollar
10. opposite; increase; decrease
11. income effect
12. normal; Normal; demand
13. inferior; substitution; income; inferior; demand
14. market
15. marginal utility; marginal utility

Important Concepts

1. Utility is a measure of satisfaction from consuming different combinations of goods. Marginal utility is the *change* in total utility.

2. False. Rationality requires only that the individual can make choices by comparing different combinations of goods, and that those choices are logically consistent or transitive. It places no restrictions on individual preferences among different goods.

3. True. The budget line is determined entirely by relative prices and income. Consumer tastes have no effect on its position or slope.

4. a. Substitution effect decreases quantity demanded; income effect decreases quantity demanded.
   b. Substitution effect—increases; income effect—decreases.

Skills and Tools

1.

| | Videos at $4 each | | Novels at $2 each | |
	Quantity	Total Expenditure on Videos	Quantity	Total Expenditure on Novels
A	0	$ 0	10	$20
B	1	4	8	16
C	2	8	6	12
D	3	12	4	8
E	4	16	2	4
F	5	20	0	0

2.

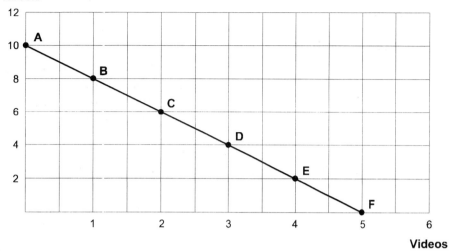

Novels / Videos

3. a. and b.

Food	Clothing	B
0	400	500
20	350	450
40	300	400
60	250	350
80	200	300
100	150	250
120	100	200
140	50	150
160	0	100

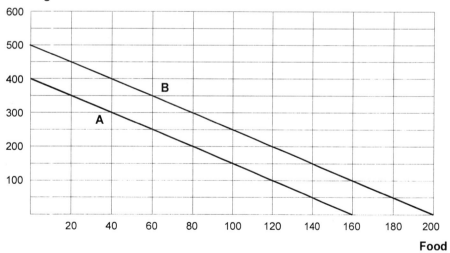

Clothing / Food

4. a and b.

Rice	Artichokes at $40	Artichokes at $20
400	0	0
320	2	4
240	4	8
160	6	12
80	8	16
0	10	20

c.

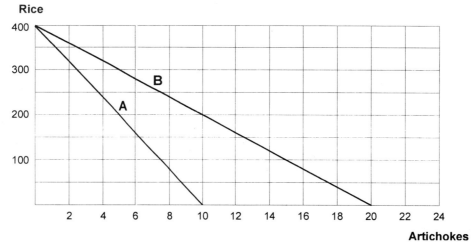

5. Yes, his preferences obey the law of diminishing marginal utility. Note from the table that each successive pair of crumpets gives Marshall ever decreasing amounts of marginal utility.

Crumpets Consumed	Total Utility	Marginal Utility
0	0	
		31
2	31	
		14
4	45	
		10
6	55	
		8
8	63	
		7
10	70	
		6
12	76	
		5
14	81	
		4
16	85	
		3
18	88	

6. a. 5; 15; greater than; oranges; apples
   b. 5; 35; greater than; apples; orange
   c. equal to; C; 6, 2

7.

Price	Quantity Demanded
$10	0
9	1/2
8	1
7	2
6	3
5	4
4	6
3	8
2	10
1	12
0	14

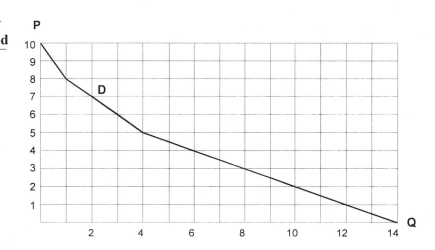

15-Minute Practice Test

Multiple Choice

1. a
2. b
3. a
4. c
5. b
6. d
7. e

8. d
9. e
10. d
11. b
12. b
13. c
14. d

True/False

1. F
2. F
3. T
4. F

5. T
6. T
7. F
8. F

ANSWERS FOR CHAPTER 6

Speaking Economics

1. business firm
2. profit
3. sole proprietorship
4. partnership
5. corporation
6. transaction costs
7. diversification
8. technology
9. production function
10. long run
11. short run
12. fixed input
13. variable input
14. total product
15. marginal product of labor
16. increasing marginal returns to labor
17. diminishing marginal returns to labor
18. law of diminishing marginal returns
19. sunk cost
20. explicit costs
21. implicit costs
22. fixed costs
23. variable costs
24. total fixed cost
25. total variable cost
26. total cost
27. average fixed cost
28. average variable cost
29. average total cost
30. marginal cost
31. long-run total cost
32. long-run average total cost
33. plant
34. economies of scale
35. diseconomies of scale
36. constant returns to scale

Chapter Highlights

1. inputs; outputs
2. production function
3. short run
4. Fixed inputs; Variable inputs
5. maximum; inputs
6. additional output; one more worker
7. diminishing; marginal product
8. opportunity cost
9. ignored
10. total cost
11. falls; rises; fall; rise; marginal cost
12. ATC, AVC (either order)
13. ATC, AVC (either order)
14. minimum
15. fixed; fixed; variable
16. least
17. less; greater; less; greater
18. short run; long run; long-run average cost (or LRATC)
19. long-run total cost; LRATC
20. long-run total cost; LRATC
21. long-run total cost; output; LRATC; flat

Important Concepts

1. (any order) gains from specialization; lower transaction costs; diversification

2. In the short run, *at least one* of the firm's inputs is fixed (i.e., does not change as the quantity of output changes). In the long run, all of the firm's inputs are variable.

3. a. Total product is the maximum output the firm can produce from a given collection of inputs; marginal product is the *change in* total product when an input (e.g., labor) increases by one unit.

b. With increasing returns to labor, an increase in output causes the marginal product of labor to rise; with diminishing returns to labor, an increase in output causes the marginal product of labor to fall.

c. Average total cost is the total cost of producing a given level of output in the short run, with given amounts of the firm's fixed inputs; long-run average total cost is the total cost of producing a given level of output in the long run, varying all inputs to use the least-cost combination.

d. Economies of scale occur when total cost rises proportionately less than output, causing the LRATC curve to slope downward; diseconomies of scale occur when total cost rises proportionately more than output, causing the LRATC curve to slope upward.

e. Diseconomies of scale—defined above—tells us that *LRATC increases* with output, when the firm varies *all* of its inputs; diminishing returns to labor tells us that the *marginal product of labor decreases* with output when the firm changes the amount of labor only, and all other inputs remain constant.

4. a. MPL
   b. AFC
   c. AVC
   d. TC
   e. AVC
   f. MC
   g. LRATC

Skills and Tools

1. a, b, c

Number of Workers	TP	MPL
0	0	
		100
1	100	
		200
2	300	
		400
3	700	
		300
4	1000	
		200
5	1200	
		100
6	1300	
		50
7	1350	

Total Product

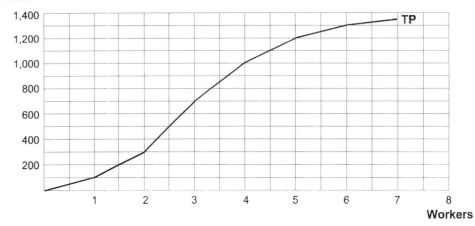

MPL

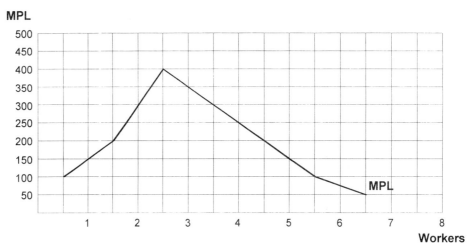

d. does; always positive; declines

2.

Number of Workers	TP	TFC $	TVC $	TC $	AFC $	AVC $	ATC $	MC $
0	0	20,000	0	20,000	— — —	— — —	— — —	
								20.0
1	100	20,000	2,000	22,000	200.0	20.0	220.0	
								10.0
2	300	20,000	4,000	24,000	66.7	13.3	80.0	
								5.0
3	700	20,000	6,000	26,000	28.6	8.6	37.1	
								6.7
4	1,000	20,000	8,000	28,000	20.0	8.0	28.0	
								10.0
5	1,200	20,000	10,000	30,000	16.7	8.3	25.0	
								20.0
6	1,300	20,000	12,000	32,000	15.4	9.2	24.6	
								40.0
7	1,350	20,000	14,000	34,000	14.8	10.4	25.2	

3.

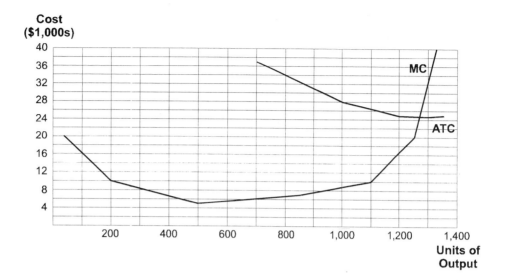

4.

Weekly Output	TFC	TVC	TC	AFC	AVC	ATC	MC
0	$100	$ 0	$ 100	– – –	– – –	– – –	
							$150
1	100	150	250	$100	$150	$250	
							130
2	100	280	380	50	140	190	
							100
3	100	380	480	33.3	126.7	160	
							20
4	100	400	500	25	100	125	
							130
5	100	530	630	20	106	126	
							130
6	100	660	760	16.7	110	126.7	
							250
7	100	910	1,010	14.3	130	144.3	
							690
8	100	1,600	1,700	12.5	200	212.5	

5. a. $50; $25; $35; $25; increasing
   b. $20; 5; 6
   c. 3; 6.5; 6; 5
   d. ATC-AVC, vertical distance; ATC curve and the AVC curve; $15; $10

6. a. Axes are labeled incorrectly—Cost should be on the vertical and output on the horizontal axis.
   b. AVC cannot exceed ATC, so the AVC and ATC curves must be labeled incorrectly.
   c. and d. By the average-marginal relationship, the MC curve must intersect the ATC curve at its minimum point and it must intersect the AVC curve at its minimum point: MC cannot be less than ATC when ATC is rising, and MC cannot be less that AVC when AVC is rising.

15-Minute Practice Test

Multiple Choice

1. e	6. e
2. e	7. b
3. e	8. e
4. b	9. c
5. e	10. a

True/False

1. F	5. F
2. F	6. T
3. F	7. T
4. F	8. F

Numerical Word Problem

1. $7,000; $9,000	5. $1; $0.83
2. $1,000; $1,000	6. $6; $6.67
3. $6,000; $8,000	7. 200
4. $7; $7.50	8. $10

ANSWERS FOR CHAPTER 7

Speaking Economics

1. accounting profit
2. economic profit
3. demand curve facing the firm
4. total revenue
5. loss
6. marginal revenue
7. marginal approach to profit
8. shutdown rule
9. exit
10. principal
11. agent
12. principal-agent problem
13. stockholder revolt
14. hostile takeover
15. friendly takeover
16. white knight
17. stock options

Chapter Highlights

1. maximize; profit
2. economic; accounting; economic
3. demand curve
4. demand curve
5. least-cost; cost
6. demand curve; technology
7. output level; output level; profit
8. one more unit of output; total revenue; output; $\Delta TR/\Delta Q$.
9. less
10. marginal revenue; marginal cost; marginal revenue; marginal cost
11. greater; less
12. TR TC (either order); TR; TC
13. marginal revenue, marginal cost (either order); MR, MC (either order).
14. revenue; cost
15. total variable cost; total variable cost
16. exit the industry
17. principal; agent
18. principal-agent; principal's

Important Concepts

1. Accounting profit = total revenue minus accounting (usually explicit) costs. Economic profit = total revenue minus *all* costs.
2. They are not the same. Marginal revenue is the *change* in total revenue caused by a one-unit increase in output.
3. The profit maximizing output level is found where the marginal cost curve crosses the marginal revenue curve *from below*.
4. Let Q* be the output level at which MR = MC. Then, in the short run, a firm should shut down whenever TR < TVC at Q*, and stay open whenever TR > TVC at Q*.
5. In a hostile takeover, outsiders who are likely to fire the current management buy the firm. In a friendly takeover, management arranges for friendly outsiders—who are *unlikely* to fire them—to buy the firm.

Skills and Tools

1. a.

Price	Output	Total Revenue
$10	0	$ 0
9	10	90
8	20	160
7	30	210
6	40	240
5	50	250
4	60	240
3	70	210
2	80	160
1	90	90
0	100	0

b. **Total Revenue ($)**

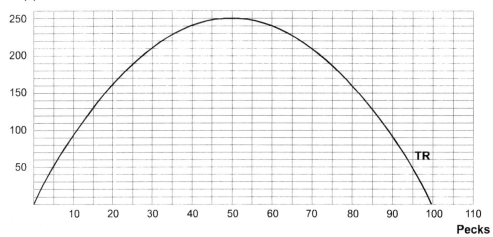

c. 50; $5; $250

2. a.

Total Revenue ($)

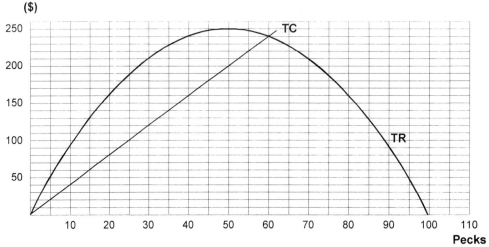

    b. $50; $80; $90; $80; $50; $0

    c. 30; $7; $210; $120; $90

3. a.

Output	Total Revenue	Marginal Revenue	Total Cost	Marginal Cost
0	$ 0		$ 50	
		$50		10
1	50		60	
		40		15
2	90		75	
		30		20
3	120		95	
		20		25
4	140		120	
		10		30
5	150		150	
		0		35
6	150		185	

    b. MR>MC; should; more

    c. MR>MC; should; more

    d. MR>MC; should; more

    e. MR<MC; should not; less

    f. MR<MC; should not; less

    g. MR<MC; should not; less

    h. 3; $25; $15; $20 (Note: To get the level of profit, compare total revenue and total cost)

4. a.

Quantity Demanded	Price	TR	MR
1	$28	28	
			24
2	26	52	
			20
3	24	72	
			16
4	22	88	
			12
5	20	100	
			8
6	18	108	
			4
7	16	112	
			0
8	14	112	
			−4
9	12	108	
			−8
10	10	100	

b. 5 bushels
c. 6 bushels
d. 7 bushels

5. a.   See the table below. To compute the entry for monthly revenue, multiply the occupancy
rate times $33,600—the revenue realized if occupancy were at 100%.

b.

Month	Occupancy Rate	TR	TVC	TFC	Profit/Loss
January	10%	3,360	4,200	11,200	−12,040
February	10%	3,360	4,200	11,200	−12,040
March	20%	6,720	4,200	11,200	−8,680
April	25%	8,400	4,200	11,200	−7,000
May	60%	20,160	4,200	11,200	4,760
June	85%	28,560	4,200	11,200	13,160
July	95%	31,920	4,200	11,200	16,520
August	95%	31,920	4,200	11,200	16,520
September	80%	26,880	4,200	11,200	11,480
October	50%	16,800	4,200	11,200	1,400
November	20%	6,720	4,200	11,200	−8,680
December	10%	3,360	4,200	11,200	−12,040

c. exceeds; total variable cost
d. Shut down for December, January, February.
     Stay open March, April, May, June, July, August, September, October, November.
e. $39,480; $3,360

15-Minute Practice Test

Multiple Choice

1. e   6. d
2. d   7. a
3. b   8. b
4. e   9. d
5. a   10. c

True/False

1. F   5. F
2. T   6. F
3. F   7. F
4. T   8. T

ANSWERS FOR CHAPTER 8

Speaking Economics

1. market structure
2. pure competition
3. price taker
4. shutdown price
5. firm's supply curve
6. market supply curve
7. normal profit
8. long-run supply curve
9. increasing cost industry
10. constant cost industry
11. decreasing cost industry
12. market signals

Chapter Highlights

1. market structure
2. standardized;
   enter into, exit from (either order)
3. price
4. cost; technology; inputs
5. price taker; price
6. price; marginal revenue curve, demand
   curve facing the firm (either order)
7. ATC; P, ATC (either order)
8. ATC; P, ATC (either order)
9. MC
10. AVC; MC; AVC; zero
11. short
12. market supply curve
13. profit, loss (either order); economic profit
    economic loss
14. zero
15. zero
16. normal
17. LRATC
18. MC; LRATC
19. long-run supply curve
20. market signals; rise; enter; fall; exit
21. right; decrease; zero

Important Concepts

1. A very large number of buyers and sellers; a standardized product offered by sellers; easy entry and exit from the market.

2. easy entry and exit

3. False. It is the demand curve facing the firm that is horizontal. The market demand curve under perfect competition will, as in any type of market, slope downward.

4. In the short run, a competitive firm should shut down whenever P < minimum AVC, and stay open whenever P > minimum AVC.

5. The market supply tells us the quantity of output supplied in the market at each price *in the short run*; the long-run supply curve tells us the quantity of output supplied at each price in the *long run*, after all long-run adjustments (e.g. entry and exit) have taken place.

6. In an increasing cost industry, an increase in industry output shifts each firm's ATC curve upward, so the long-run supply curve slopes upward. In a decreasing cost industry, an increase in industry output shifts each firm's ATC curve downward, so the long-run supply curve slopes downward. In a constant cost industry, changes in industry output have no affect on each firm's ATC curve, so the long-run supply curve is horizontal.

Skills and Tools

1. a. and b.

Output	TR	TC	MR	MC	Profit
0	0	6			−6
			12	1	
1	12	7			5
			12	3	
2	24	10			14
			12	5	
3	36	15			21
			12	7	
4	48	22			26
			12	9	
5	60	31			29
			12	11	
6	72	42			30
			12	13	
7	84	55			29
			12	15	
8	96	70			26
			12	17	
9	108	87			21
			12	19	
10	120	106			14

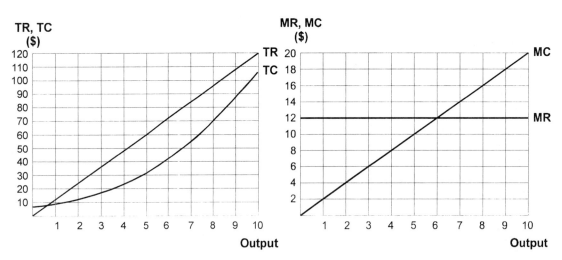

c. 6; $30; vertical; 6; less than; greater than; 6; equal to

2. a. 7; $15; $105
   b. increasing; 7.5; rise; 20 and 25; rise; 150 and 188
   c. keep producing; exceeds; 6; negative
   d. is not; shut down

3.

Market Price	Quantity Supplied
$70	7.8
60	7.5
50	7
40	6.5
30	6
20	5 or 0
10	0
5	0

4. a. 20; 40; 60; 0
   b. 400; 800; 1,200 (See graph.) Equilibrium price is $250.
   c. 600; 1,200; 1,800 (See graph.) Equilibrium price is $200.
   d. 0; 800; 1,600 (See graph.) Equilibrium price is $100.

5. a. $10; is not; positive profit; enter this market; shift market supply to the right; fall
   b. $4; is not; negative profit; exit this market; shift market supply to the left; rise
   c. $6; earn zero economic profit; neither enter nor exit; will

15-Minute Practice Test

Multiple Choice

1. a	6. d
2. b	7. b
3. d	8. e
4. a	9. d
5. c	10. c

True/False

1. F	5. F
2. F	6. F
3. T	7. T
4. T	8. T

ANSWERS FOR CHAPTER 9

Speaking Economics

1. monopoly firm
2. monopoly market
3. natural monopoly
4. patent
5. copyright
6. government franchise
7. rent-seeking activity
8. single-price monopoly
9. price discrimination
10. perfect price discrimination

Chapter Highlights

1. close substitutes
2. economies of scale; cost per unit
   (or average cost)
3. monopoly; economic profit; lower
4. maximize profit
5. technology; inputs; demand
6. marginal revenue; marginal revenue
7. negative
8. MC; MC; below
9. ATC; ATC
10. AVC; MC
11. long
12. negative
13. price; output
14. higher; lower; lower; higher
15. rent-seeking activity; profit
16. increasing; increasing; larger
17. costs
18. perfect
19. perfect; demand

Important Concepts

1. economies of scale; control of a scarce input; government franchise; protection of intellectual property (or patents and copyrights)

2. No. The result is the same for the short run—economic profit may exist. But in a monopoly—unlike a competitive firm—the firm may also earn economic profit in the long run.

3. Government regulation; rent-seeking activity

4. False. A monopoly, like any firm, will produce an output level where MR = MC, and will want to charge the price that enables it to sell that output level. Raising its price higher than this would decrease its profit.

5. A downward-sloping demand curve; the ability to identify consumers willing to pay more than others; and the ability to prevent low-price customers from reselling to high-price customers.

6. False. A monopoly firm has no supply curve.

Skills and Tools

1. a. b.

P	Q^D	TR	MR
$20	0	$ 0	
			$18
18	1	18	
			14
16	2	32	
			10
14	3	42	
			6
12	4	48	
			2
10	5	50	
			−2
8	6	48	
			−6
6	7	42	
			−10
4	8	32	
			−14
2	9	18	
			−18
0	10	0	

c. positive; increase
d. negative; decrease
e. negative; 5

2. a. and b.

P	Q	TR	MR
$120	0	$ 0	
			$105
105	5	525	
			75
90	10	900	
			30
60	20	1,200	
			−30
30	30	900	
			−90
0	40	0	

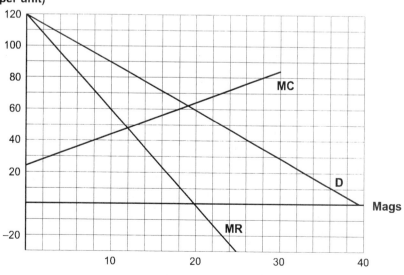

   c. 12; $50; $50; $84

   d. less than; fall

3. a. 40

   b. $300; $300; equal to

   c. $500

   d. $400

   e. $100

   f. $4,000

4. Graph for a., b., and d.

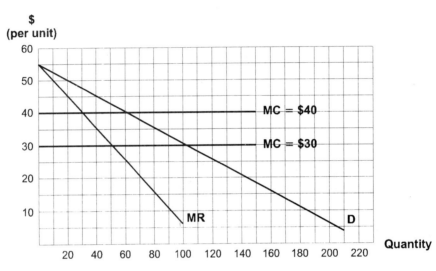

   c. 52; $43. (To get these exact, set the equation for MR equal to MC = $30. Solve for Q. Plug Q into the demand equation to get price.)

   d. 32; $48 (To get these exact, use the equation for MR equal to MC = $40. Solve for Q. Plug Q into the demand equation to get price.)

   e. $5; not to

5. a. a; –b; a/b

   b. a; –2b; a/2b

   c.

Demand	Marginal Revenue
P = 34 – 4Q	MR = 34 – 8Q
P = 28 – 15Q	MR = 28 – 30Q
P = 72 – 12Q	MR = 72 – 24Q
P = 12 – 8Q	MR = 12 – 16Q
P = 105 – 25Q	MR = 105 – 50Q

6. a. and b.

P	QD
$1,000	0
750	1
500	2
250	3
0	4

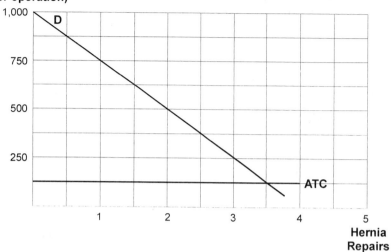

c. 3; $750; $375; $325
d. 3; $750 + $500 + $250 = $1,500; $375; $1,125
e. He makes more profit when he price discriminates.

15-Minute Practice Test

Multiple Choice

1. b
2. a
3. c
4. b
5. d

6. e
7. d
8. c
9. b
10. e

True/False

1. F
2. F
3. F
4. F

5. F
6. F
7. T
8. F

ANSWERS FOR CHAPTER 10

Speaking Economics

1. monopolistic competition
2. nonprice competition
3. oligopoly
4. minimum efficient scale (MES)
5. game theory
6. payoff matrix
7. dominant strategy
8. duopoly
9. repeated play
10. explicit collusion
11. cartel
12. tacit collusion
13. tit for tat
14. price leadership

Chapter Highlights

1. (either order) perfect competition, monopoly; perfectly competitive; perfect competition
2. (either order) buyers, sellers; (either order) entry, exit; differentiated
3. differentiated; downward; decline
4. short; long; zero
5. excess; minimum
6. cutting its price; nonprice
7. interdependent
8. dominant
9. zero economic profit

Important Concepts

1. a. differentiated product
   b. no significant barriers to entry or exit. (Could also answer "many firms," although monopolistic competition generally has fewer firms than pure competition.)

2. False. While it is true that under monopolistic competition there are many firms, each one produces a differentiated product, so it faces a downward sloping demand curve.

3. There is strategic interaction in oligopoly, but not in monopolistic competition.

4. (any order) economies of scale; reputation; strategic barriers; government created barriers

5. Both are examples of cooperative behavior designed to increase oligopolists' profits. But while explicit collusion involves direct communication and explicit agreements between competitive firms to set prices, tacit collusion occurs without direct communication or explicit agreements.

6. a. oligopoly
   b. monopoly
   c. monopolistic competition
   d. pure competition

7. False. While it *may* raise the price, it could also lower the price by enabling firms to produce and sell more output and lower their cost per unit.

8. Table:

Characteristic	Perfect Competition	Monopolistic Competition	Oligopoly	Monopoly
Number of Firms	very many	many	few	one
Type of Output	identical	differentiated	identical or differentiated	not applicable
View of Pricing	price taker	price setter	price setter	price setter
Barriers to Entry or Exit?	no	no	yes	yes
Strategic Interdependence?	no	no	yes	no
How profit-maximizing output level is found	MC = MR	MC = MR	through strategic inter-dependence	MC = MR
Possible values for short-run profit	positive, negative, or zero	positive, negative, or zero	positive, negative, or zero	positive, negative, or zero
Possible values for long-run profit	zero	zero	positive or zero	positive or zero
Is Advertising Expected?	never	almost always	yes, if product is differentiated	sometimes

Skills and Tools

1. a. can; maximize profit; where marginal revenue equals marginal cost
   b. 20; $6; $5; 20 × (6 − 5) = $20
   c. enter; enter; shift leftward; zero

2. a. 25; $12; 4,000; 160; perfect competition
   b. 4,000; $4; 12,000; 3; oligopoly
   c. 12,000; $8; 8,000; 1; natural monopoly

3. a.

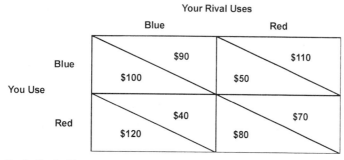

   b. Red; Red; Yes
   c. Red; Red; Yes
   d. Red; Red
   e. Yes; Blue; Blue
   f. $100; $120; When I cheat.
   g. $90; $110; When she cheats.

4. a. $20; 5: zero
   b. 400; 4 bushels

  c. greater than; positive
  d. $15; exceed
  e. $20; 5; zero

15-Minute Practice Test

Multiple Choice

1. b
2. c
3. d
4. c
5. c

6. e
7. d
8. a
9. e
10. b

True/False

1. F
2. T
3. F
4. F

5. F
6. F
7. T
8. T

ANSWERS FOR CHAPTER 11

Speaking Economics

1. product markets
2. factor markets
3. perfectly competitive labor market
4. derived demand
5. wage taker
6. marginal revenue product (MRP)
7. market labor demand curve
8. substitute input
9. substitute input
10. reservation wage
11. labor supply curve
12. long-run labor supply curve
13. labor shortage
14. labor surplus

Chapter Highlights

1. product (or output) market
2. derived
3. (perfectly) competitive; wage taker
4. technology; price; wage rate
5. total revenue
6. marginal product of labor
7. MRP; W; MRP; W
8. (either order) MRP, W; MRP; wage
9. downward; labor demand; wage rate
10. (either order) MRP, W; downward; increase
11. wage rate; summing
12. rightward; leftward
13. complementary; substitutable
14. complementary; substitutable
15. wage taker
16. greater
17. shift
18. leftward
19. leftward; rightward
20. long-run labor supply curve; acquire new skills
21. more
22. equilibrium; intersect
23. labor supply; labor supply
24. market signals; overshoot; overshooting
25. shortage; surplus

Important Concepts

1. (any order) a great many buyers and sellers of labor in the market; all workers in the labor market appear the same to firms; no barriers to entering or leaving the labor market

2. False. In a competitive labor market, all firms are wage takers—they can hire as many workers as they wish at the prevailing market wage.

3. The special formula is $MRP = MPL \times P$.

4. (any order) any three of the following four
   a. a decrease in the price of *output* (for many firms in the same labor market)
   b. a change in the price of some other input (an increase in the price of a complementary input or a decrease in the price of a substitute input)
   c. a technological change (specifically, the use of a new input which is substitutable for labor
   d. a decrease in the number of firms

5. (any order) any three of the following four
   a. a change in tastes toward work in that market
   b. a decrease in the wage in some *other* labor market
   c. a decrease in the cost of acquiring human capital needed to qualify in that labor market
   d. an increase in population in that labor market

6. The long run labor supply curve would become steeper, since a wage change would cause less entry or exit of workers than would be the case without the law.

Skills and Tools

1. a.

Quantity of Labor	Total Product	Marginal Product of Labor (MPL)	Price per Sandwich	Total Revenue	Marginal Revenue Product (MRP)	Wage (W)
0	0		$4	$0		$50
		30			$120	
1	30		4	120		50
		40			160	
2	70		4	280		50
		30			120	
3	100		4	400		50
		20			80	
4	120		4	480		50
		10			40	
5	130		4	520		50
		−10			−40	
6	120		4	480		50

b.   MRP; wage; hiring the additional worker; yes; yes; yes; 4

2. a.

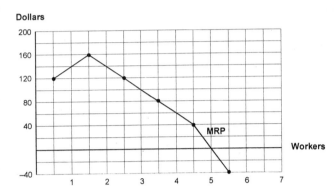

b.   3; 4

3. a.

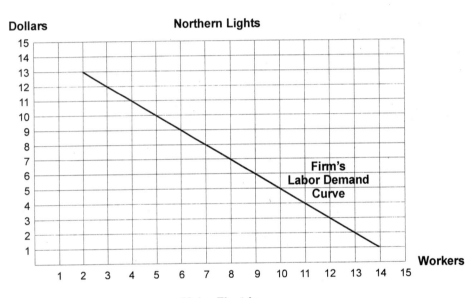

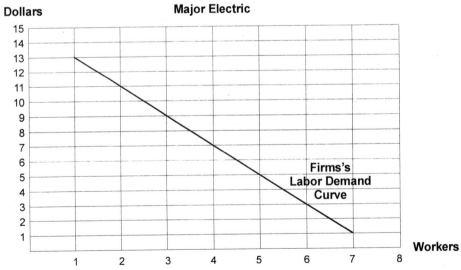

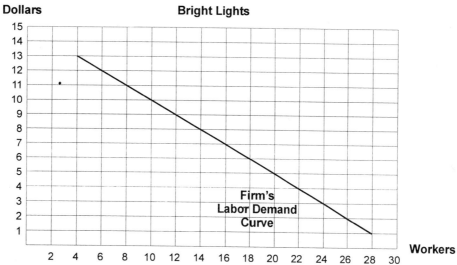

Dollars   **Bright Lights**

Firm's Labor Demand Curve

Workers

b. **Dollars**   **Market for Lamp Workers**

LD

Workers

c.   14; 4; 2; 8
d.   42; 12; 6; 24

4. a.   2; 4; cause a movement along the labor supply curve
    b.   Equilibrium wage is $80
       5 translators employed

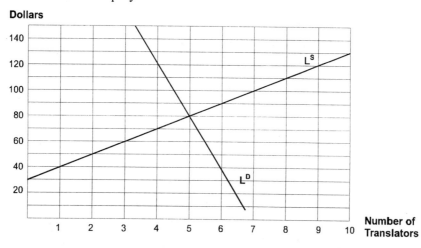

Dollars

L^S

L^D

Number of Translators

5. a. Equilibrium wage is $25;
       5,000 EAs/RAs hired
   b. They hire 15 EAs/RAs this year. (Hint: They keep hiring until what equals what?)

6. a.

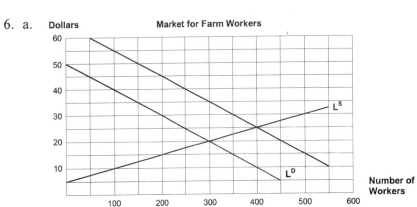

   b. $20; 300
   c. increase; increase; demand curve; rightward
   d. (See graph.) demand curve; $25; 400
   e. higher; mover to; seek employment; lower; higher

15-Minute Practice Test

Multiple Choice

1. a	6. d
2. e	7. d
3. b	8. e
4. c	9. d
5. d	10. c

True/False

1. F	5. T
2. F	6. F
3. T	7. T
4. F	8. T

ANSWERS FOR CHAPTER 12

Speaking Economics

1. compensating wage differential
2. non-monetary job characteristic
3. discrimination
4. statistical discrimination
5. property income
6. transfer payment
7. poverty rate
8. poverty line
9. Lorenz curve
10. Gini coefficient

Chapter Highlights

1. compensating; equally attractive
2. nonmonetary; compensating; higher
3. compensating; higher
4. human; compensating; higher
5. higher
6. increase; decrease
7. employers
8. (any order) employees, customers
9. over; under
10. one; greater
11. poverty rate
12. fair

Important Concepts

1. (in any order)
   a. nonmonetary job characteristics
   b. cost of living differences
   c. differences in human capital

2. (in any order)
   a. barriers to entry (e.g., union wage setting)
   b. discrimination
   c. differences in ability

3. (in any order)
   a. employers—market forces discourage discrimination
   b. employees—market forces encourage discrimination
   c. customers—market forces encourage discrimination

4. (three of the following four, in any order)
   a. Earned income progressive income taxes; leads to an overestimate of inequality
   b. Earned income ignores transfer payments (and transfers in kind); leads to an overestimate of inequality
   c. earned income ignores fringe benefits; leads to an underestimate of inequality
   d. earned income ignores capital gains; leads to an underestimate of inequality

5. (in any order)
   a. covered, unskilled workers: wages rate increases, employment decreases
   b. uncovered, unskilled workers: wage rate decreases, employment increases
   c. skilled workers: wage rate increases, employment increases

Skills and Tools

1. a. $15; $10
   b. the same as; the same as; the same as; higher wage industry; lower wage industry; true
   c. $12.50; $12.50 (Hint: If employers view all workers the same, and if workers choose where to work only by the wage they receive, then the common equilibrium wage must equate *total* labor demand on the island to *total* labor supply on the island)
   d. better off; worse off; no

2. a.

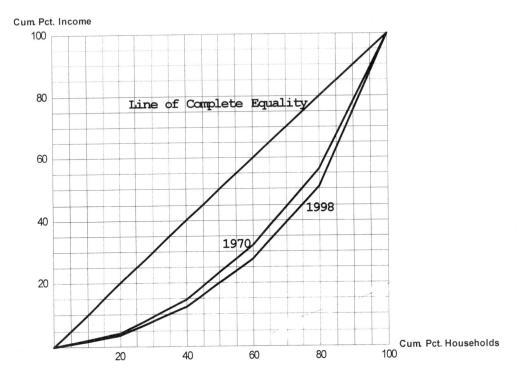

Cum Pct. Income

Line of Complete Equality

1998

1970

Cum Pct. Households

b. more; increased

3. a. $210,000
   b.

Family	Percent of Population	Cumulative Percent of Population	Ordered Income (Lowest to (Highest)	Percent of Income	Cumulative Percent of Income
G	10%	10%	$ 4,000	2%	2%
E	10%	20%	6,000	3%	5%
H	10%	30%	8,000	4%	9%
F	10%	40%	13,000	6%	15%
D	10%	50%	18,000	9%	23%
B*	10%	60%	27,000	13%	36%
I	10%	70%	27,000	13%	49%
J	10%	80%	27,000	13%	62%
A*	10%	90%	40,000	19%	81%
C	10%	100%	40,000	19%	100%

*Note: Families B, I, and J can appear in any order; as can families A and C.

   c. $9,000; three families; 30%

d.

**Cumulative Percent
of Income**

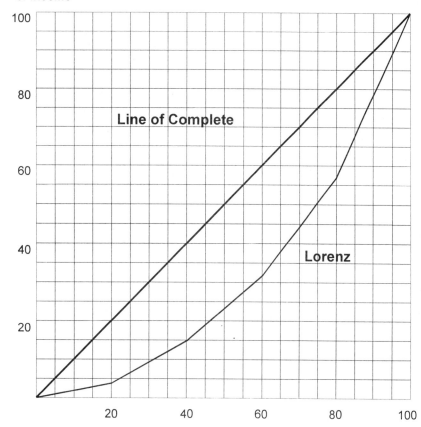

**Cumulative Percent
of Households**

15-Minute Practice Test

Multiple Choice

1. b	6. c
2. a	7. c
3. b	8. c
4. e	9. e
5. a	10. d

True/False

1. T	5. F
2. T	6. T
3. T	7. F
4. T	8. F

ANSWERS FOR CHAPTER 13

Speaking Economics

1. marginal revenue product of capital
2. present value
3. discounting
4. discount rate
5. principle of asset valuation
6. general human capital
7. specific human capital
8. financial asset
9. bond
10. principal (or face value)
11. maturity date
12. pure discount bond
13. coupon payments
14. yield
15. primary market
16. secondary market
17. share of stock
18. mutual fund
19. dividend
20. capital gain
21. Dow Jones Industrial Average
22. Standard & Poor's 500
23. fundamental analysis
24. technical analysis
25. efficient market

Chapter Highlights

1. interest; interest; more
2. today's
3. $Y / (1 + i)^n$
4. larger; later
5. present values
6. rises; rise
7. lower; higher
8. general; general
9. specific; specific
10. present value
11. physical; inversely (or negatively); greater; more
12. lower; lower
13. prices; price
14. primary
15. higher; lower; lower; lower; higher
16. present value; the number of shares outstanding
17. increase; increase; decrease; decrease decrease
18. fundamental; technical

Important Concepts

1. General human capital is valuable at many firms, and is generally acquired and paid for by workers themselves. Specific human capital is valuable primarily at one specific firm, and is generally provided and paid for by the firm.

2. False. A bond promises to pay a fixed amount or fixed amounts at future dates. The only way the interest rate or yield can be higher is if the price is *lower*.

3. A rise in the interest rate decreases the total present value of the additional revenue from any given piece of capital. Therefore, as the interest rate rises, some pieces of capital will no longer justify their cost, and firms will decide not to buy them. Thus, as the interest rate rises, investment spending on physical capital in the economy decreases.

4. (in any order)
   a. facilitates large scale production
   b. enables the reallocation of spending across time
   c. reduces risk
   d. disciplines management

Skills and Tools

1. PV of $1 received n years in the future, given interest rate i

	Years (n)					
	1	**2**	**3**	**4**	**5**	**20**
5%	0.95	0.91	0.86	0.82	0.78	0.38
10%	0.91	0.83	0.75	0.68	0.62	0.15
15%	0.87	0.76	0.66	0.57	0.50	0.06
20%	0.83	0.69	0.58	0.48	0.40	0.03

Interest Rate (i)

2. a. $2 million; $1.9 million; $1.82 million; $1.56 million; $ 0.76 million
   b. $2 million; $1.74 million; $1.52 million; $1 million; $0.12 million
   c. $1.544 million
   d. $0.720 million

3. a. 7,600; 7,280; 6,880; 21,760.
   b. 7,280; 6,640; 6,000; 19,920.
   c. (See table.)
   d. definitely; exceeds; definitely; exceeds; definitely; exceeds; definitely not; fall short; 3.
   e. buy; buy; not buy; 2.
   f. fewer.

Computer	Additional Annual Revenue	Total Present Value with a discount rate of:	
		5%	**10%**
1	$8,000	$21,760	$19,920
2	$5,000	$13,600	$12,450
3	$2,000	$5,440	$4,980
4	$1,000	$2,720	$2,490

4. a. 820; 820; 24 (or 25).
   b. 680; 680; 29 (or 30).

5. a. 40,000,000; 72.73.
   b. lower than.

c. lower than.
d. higher than.

15-Minute Practice Test

Multiple Choice

1. d
2. b
3. d
4. e
5. b

6. a
7. b
8. d
9. c
10. b

True/False

1. F
2. F
3. T
4. T

5. F
6. T
7. F
8. F

ANSWERS FOR CHAPTER 14

Speaking Economics

1. Pareto improvement
2. economic efficiency

3. productive efficiency
4. allocative efficiency

Chapter Highlights

1. economic efficiency
2. fair
3. better off; harms no one
4. Pareto improvement
5. side payment
6. productively
7. productively
8. productive
9. productive; allocated
10. (perfectly) competitive
11. profit; perfectly competitive

12. economic
13. allocatively; Pareto
14. market demand curve
15. market supply curve
16. benefit; cost (either order)
17. benefit, cost (either order); equilibrium
18. productively; allocatively
19. marginal cost
20. imperfectly competitive; greater; little; high
21. imperfectly competitive; price
    discrimination; Pareto improvements

Important Concepts

1. a. Pareto improvement
   b. Pareto improvement
   c. not a Pareto improvement (someone is harmed—you)

2. For an imperfectly competitive firm, price is greater than MC. The price is what someone is willing to pay for one more unit of the good (the marginal benefit to some consumer); MC is the additional cost of producing one more unit to some firm. Since some consumer is willing to pay more than the marginal cost to some firm, both the firm and the consumer could be made better off if one more unit of the good were produced.

3. (any order) full employment of resources; each firm produces maximum output from resources available to it; the allocation of inputs among firms produces the maximum total output.

4. False. The statement is backwards. A true statement is that productive efficiency is necessary for economic efficiency. When there is allocative inefficiency, the economy will be economically inefficient, but could still be productively efficient.

5. No, the economy is *not* productively efficient. Proof: It we move a unit of labor from firm B to firm A, then output will decrease by 3 units at firm B but increase by 5 units at firm A. The economy's output of this good will thus rise by 2 units. This is an increase in production without any decrease in the production of any other good. But in a productively efficiency economy, all such possibilities have already been exploited.

6. a. productive inefficiency
   b. allocative inefficiency
   c. productive inefficiency

Skills and Tools

1. a. $18; $6; greater than; is not; could; could not
   b. $10; $10; equal to; is; could not; could not
   c. $4; $13; less than; is not; could not; could

2. a.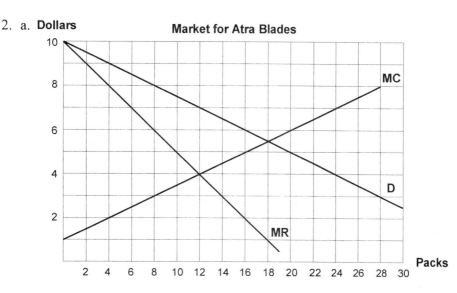

Market for Atra Blades

b.   marginal revenue equals marginal cost; 12; $7
c. $7; $4; does not
d.   18 thousand packs; equal to

3. a.

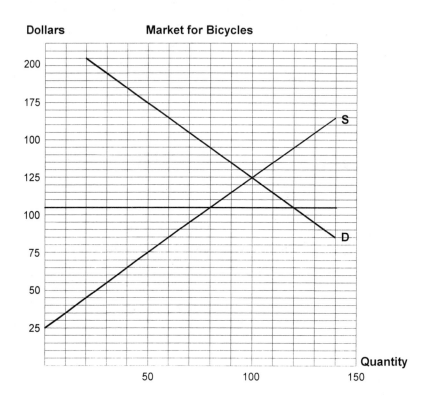

b. $125; 100
c.   (See graph.)
d.   fewer; lower; fewer; lower
e. $145; $105; is greater than; is not

15-Minute Practice Test

Multiple Choice

1. a	6. e
2. d	7. b
3. d	8. c
4. a	9. c
5. c	10. c

True/False

1. T	5. F
2. T	6. T
3. F	7. F
4. F	8. F

ANSWERS FOR CHAPTER 15

Speaking Economics

1. tort
2. market failure
3. average cost pricing
4. Averich-Johnson effect
5. externality
6. public good

7. private good
8. rivalry
9. excludability
10. tragedy of the commons
11. Herfindahl-Hirschman index

Chapter Highlights

1. criminal
2. property; property; Pareto; property; inefficient
3. Contracts; contracts; exchange
4. regulatory; efficient
5. efficient
6. marginal benefit; marginal cost; little
7. excise; marginal cost
8. inefficiency
9. LRATC, demand (either order); zero
10. by-product
11. marginal costs; marginal benefits

12. (either order) social cost, private cost
13. marginal benefits; marginal cost
14. (either order) social benefit, private benefit
15. (private) market
16. (either order): rivalry, excludability; rivalry; excludability
17. free riders
18. (private) market; government
19. zero
20. Anti-trust law or Anti-trust policy; mergers
21. regulation; regulation

Important Concepts

1. (any order) criminal; property; contract; tort; antitrust

2. False. An income tax introduces inefficiencies of its own by altering the behavior of workers and firms in the labor market, and moving the labor market away from the efficient outcome.

3. (any order) externalities (positive and negative); imperfect competition; public goods

4. a. (negative) externality
    b. imperfect competition
    c. (positive) externality
    d. public good

5. a. (either order) rivalry, excludability
    b. (either order) nonrivalry, nonexcludability

Skills and Tools

1. a.

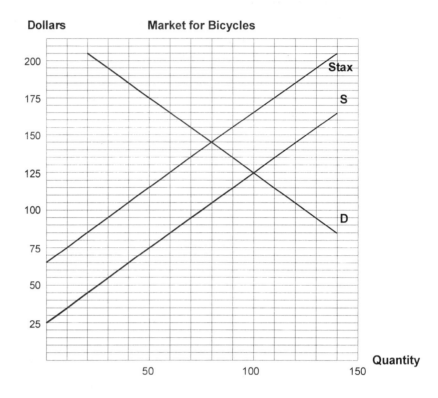

b. $125; 100
c. (See graph.)
d. $145; $105; 80
e. risen; $20; fallen; $20; $40; just equal to
f. $145; $105; is greater than; is not

2. a natural monopoly
   b. (See graph.)

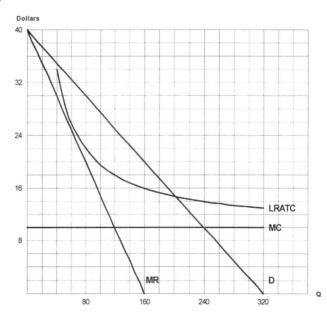

c. 120; $25; 18; $8,400

d. is not; 25; 10; can;

e. 10 cents; 240 thousand; would; suffer a loss; $9,600; only if the firm also receives a subsidy to cover its losses.

f. 200; 15; 0; higher than; lower than.

g. greater than; less than; lower than.

3. a.

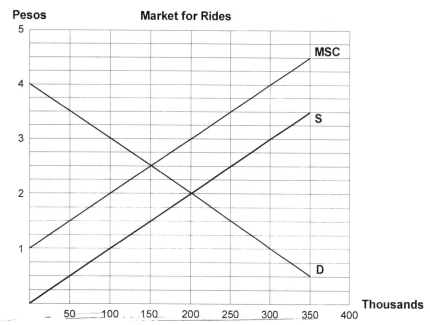

b. 2; 200

c. is not; too high; less than

d. levy a tax of 1 peso per ride on Jeeneys; raise; supply; leftward; increase; 2.5 pesos; decrease; 150

e. will; equal to

4. a. Industry A: 2,950
Industry B: 4,000
Industry C: 2,500

b. Indusry B is the most concentrated.

5. a. 1850

b. 2450; 600

c. would

15-Minute Practice Test

Multiple Choice

1. d

2. d

3. a

4. e

5. e

6. c

7. a

8. d

9. c

10. e

True/False

1. F   5. T
2. T   6. F
3. F   7. F
4. F   8. T

ANSWERS FOR CHAPTER 16

Speaking Economics

1. exports   6. exchange rate
2. imports   7. tariff
3. absolute advantage   8. quota
4. comparative advantage 9. protectionism
5. terms of trade

Chapter Highlights

1. with fewer resources; at a lower opportunity cost
2. comparative advantage; less
3. opportunity costs; absolute
4. specialize
5. natural resources; natural resources
6. comparative advantages; past

7. producers; Consumers
8. producers; Consumers
9. reduce; raise; producers; consumers; loses; reduce; decrease
10. decrease; raise; decrease; increased government revenue
11. comparative advantage

Important Concepts

1. A country has an absolute advantage in producing some good when it can produce it *using fewer resources* than some other country. A country has a comparative advantage in producing some good when it can produce it at a *lower opportunity cost*, in terms of other goods foregone, than some other country. Comparative advantage determines which goods and services a nation will produce and export.

2. (any three of the following four):
   a. high costs of trading, e.g., transportation costs
   b. country is large relative to its trading partners
   c. increasing, rather than constant, opportunity costs
   d. government barriers to trade, e.g., tariffs or quotas

3.

	Country A		Country B	
	Producers of:	Consumers of:	Producers of:	Consumers of:
Good X	gain	lose	lose	gain
Good Y	lose	gain	gain	lose

4. No, the total gains are greater than the total losses, so the world as a whole benefits. We know this because, when trade opens up, and nations produce and export according to their comparative advantages, total world production increases. Thus, total world consumption increases, so the world is better off.

5.

	Country A		Country B	
	Producers of:	Consumers of:	Producers of:	Consumers of:
Good Y	gain	lose	lose	gain

6. The infant industry argument is that a nation may *eventually* have a comparative advantage in producing some good, but that the industry may not be able to develop on its own without help from the government. This is especially the case in less developed economies where new industries may have difficulty obtaining the needed financing. The infant industry argument is an argument *for* protectionism.

7. False. First, a low-wage country is not necessarily a low-cost country. Wages may be low in a country in part because workers are less productive there (say, because they have less capital with which to work). Second, even when one country has lower wages *and* lower costs for all goods than another country, the high wage country will still have a *comparative* advantage in producing some goods. Thus, the high wage country will still gain from producing and exporting those goods.

Skills and Tools

1. a. 400; 200; 2; bicycles; 2; bicycles
   b. 900; 300; 3; bicycles; 3; bicycles
   c. Opportunity Costs

	Per Bicycle	Per VCR
Germany	1/2 VCR	2 bicycles
United States	1/3 VCR	3 bicycles

   d. VCRs; bicycles; VCRs; bicycles

2. a. VCRs; bicycles; bicycles; VCRs; VCRs; bicycles; bicycles; VCRs

   b.

	Bicycle Production	VCR Production
Germany	−50	+25
United States	+60	−20
World	+10	+5

c. The Gains from Specialization and Trade

	Production	Loss from exports (–) or gain from imports (+)	Net Gain
Germany			
Bicycles	–50	+55	–5
VCRs	25	–22	3
United States			
Bicycles	60	–55	5
VCRs	–20	+22	2

d. 2.5; both Germany and the United States; 5; 2; 5; 3

3. a.

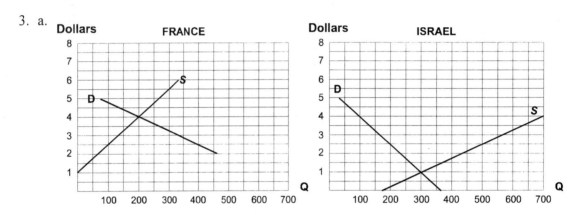

b. $4; 200; $1; 300
c. import; export
d. fall; rise; increase; decrease; rise; decrease; increase
e. lower; better off; lower; worse off; higher; worse off; higher; better off

4. Quantity of French orange imports = 800 – 200P
    Quantity of Israeli orange exports = 200P – 200
    Free trade equilibrium price is $2.5 per kilo.

15-Minute Practice Test

Multiple Choice

1. c		6. d
2. a		7. d
3. a		8. e
4. c		9. c
5. e		10. a

True/False

1. F		5. T
2. F		6. T
3. F		7. F
4. F		8. F

costs for all goods than another country, the high wage country will still have a *comparative* advantage in producing some goods. Thus, the high wage country will still gain from producing and exporting those goods.

Skills and Tools

1. a. 400; 200; 2; bicycles; 2; bicycles
   b. 900; 300; 3; bicycles; 3; bicycles
   c. Opportunity Costs

	Per Bicycle	Per VCR
Germany	1/2 VCR	2 bicycles
United States	1/3 VCR	3 bicycles

   d. VCRs; bicycles; VCRs; bicycles

2. a. VCRs; bicycles; bicycles; VCRs; VCRs; bicycles; bicycles; VCRs

   b.

	Bicycle Production	VCR Production
Germany	−50	+25
United States	+60	−20
World	+10	+5

   c. The Gains from Specialization and Trade

	Production	Loss from exports (−) or gain from imports (+)	Net Gain
Germany			
Bicycles	−50	+55	−5
VCRs	25	−22	3
United States			
Bicycles	60	−55	5
VCRs	−20	+22	2

   d. 2.5; both Germany and the United States; 5; 2; 5; 3

3. a.

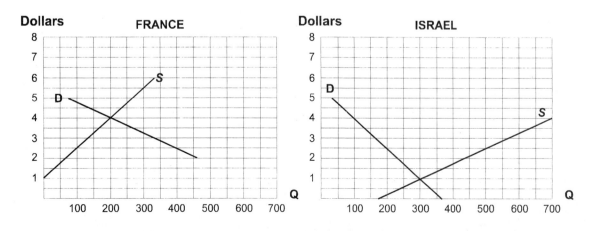

b. $4; 200; $1; 300
c. import; export
d. fall; rise; increase; decrease; rise; decrease; increase
e. lower; better off; lower; worse off; higher; worse off; higher; better off

4. Quantity of French orange imports = 800 − 200P
Quantity of Israeli orange exports = 200P − 200
Free trade equilibrium price is $2.5 per kilo.

15-Minute Practice Test

Multiple Choice

1. c		6. d
2. a		7. d
3. a		8. e
4. c		9. c
5. e		10. a

True/False

1. F		5. T
2. F		6. T
3. F		7. F
4. F		8. F